A Do-It-at-Home Retreat

André Ravier, S.J.

A Do-It-at-Home Retreat

The Spiritual Exercises of St. Ignatius of Loyola
According to the "Nineteenth Annotation"

Translated by
Cornelius Michael Buckley, S.J.

IGNATIUS PRESS   SAN FRANCISCO

Title of the French original:
En Retraite chez soi
© 1989 Ateliers Henry Labat
Vie Chrétienne, Paris

Cover art: stained glass window
Saint Ignatius Church, San Francisco
Cover design by Marcia Ryan

With ecclesiastical approval
© 1991 Ignatius Press, San Francisco
ISBN 0-89870-363-8
Library of Congress catalogue number 90-85500
Printed in the United States of America

"Whenever you pray, go to your room, close your door, and pray to your Father in private."

(Matt 6:6)

To regulate my life
more
according to the loving plan
of my Father
who is in heaven

CONTENTS

7

PREFACE

This book is designed for priests, religious, and laymen who sincerely want to place themselves "face to face" with God so as to order their lives along his loving designs but who, because of professional or familial commitments or for any other reason, cannot go off somewhere to follow the Spiritual Exercises of St. Ignatius for three, eight, ten, or thirty days. Provided these individuals put aside one or two hours of silence each day at home for a week (a month would be better), they can still make an excellent retreat.[1] It is vitally important, however, that these individual retreatants place themselves under the direction of a competent spiritual guide, with whom they can converse in complete confidence, one who knows the Spiritual Exercises well and who will explain to them how God is dealing with their soul and who will accompany them in their search for the true love of God.

This is how Ignatius, Peter Favre, and their first companions gave the Spiritual Exercises.

---

[1] See p. 233 for an eight-day retreat plan.

TRANSLATOR'S NOTE

In a footnote not cited in this English edition, Father Ravier advised his readers that he relied, for the most part, on the Jerusalem Bible for his Scriptural citations in his original work. He stated, however, that when he judged it advisable he had no qualms about using other French translations and that on occasion, rejecting all translations, he had recourse to the original Greek rendition of the New Testament. The translator has been guided by the same principle. Although he has restricted himself to the English translations of *The Jerusalem Bible* (1966) and *The New American Bible* (1970) for Scriptural citations and has, for the most part, relied on the author's modified renditions of the standard French translations of *The Spiritual Exercises* by François Courel (1960) and Edouard Gueydan (1985), he has at times had recourse to the so-called *versio prima* of 1541, and whenever possible he has tried to fit in the English translations of Joseph Rickaby (1923) and Louis J. Puhl (1951).

After saying this, Jesus raised his eyes to heaven and said:

> "... *Eternal life is this:*
> *to know you**
> *the only true God,*
> *and Jesus Christ,*
> *whom you have sent.*"

(John 17:3)

---

*Knowledge in the Biblical sense does not come from a purely intellectual process but from a living experience involving the whole person. It consists in an enlightenment of the mind and an attraction of the will, an effort on the part of the intellect and a commitment on the part of the will. When knowledge matures it becomes love.

INTRODUCTION

The Spiritual Exercises by St. Ignatius of Loyola is quite obviously the book that has inspired this *Do-It-at-Home Retreat*. The plan we have carried out in this book in the pages that follow goes along with Ignatius' thinking. Did not he himself foresee that a person could make a retreat, in the true sense of the term, at home without ever interrupting his daily routine? And did not he indicate in his directives and annotations that the retreat should be adapted to the particular circumstances of the retreatant?

A retreat should be made in an atmosphere of complete spiritual freedom, under the inspiration of the Holy Spirit. This is why every retreat (irrespective of where it is made) is basically a personal experience.

We have kept intact the following points from St. Ignatius' *Spiritual Exercises:*

— First of all, there is the primary purpose of the Exercises, namely, to turn from sin (or tepidity) to the good or the better.

— The necessary essentials, among which are, first and foremost, a fundamental "indifference"—that is, a freedom from everything that is not God, a resolute submission to his providential plan for me.

— The gradual unfolding of the order found in the Exercises: the four "Weeks", or stages, going from the Foundation and following through to the Contemplation to Attain and Live in the Love of God.

— The election, that is, the choice I make during the course of this spiritual experience to give order or an orientation to my life's direction.

— The principal themes and texts.

— The personal interchange between the retreatant and the spiritual director. This "touching base" with one another should take place at the very least occasionally, or, if it is necessary, it can take place by correspondence.

Despite their unique character, St. Ignatius' Spiritual Exercises contain no particular spiritual *doctrine*. Rather, they present an art of teaching spiritual *experience* (either conversion or spiritual progress). They plot out the sure course, the dangers and illusions, the various conditions, the helps, and the impediments for attaining this end—all the while respecting God's complete liberty as well as the freedom of the soul of the person making the retreat. *Essentially* the Christian experience is the same for all, but it takes on a personal form for each one. We have taken from this pedagogical method the explanations, advice, and counsels (even those that are meant exclusively for the director) and have been faithful in recording them here.

The "retreat" we propose is an "immersion" (*immersion* connotes baptism) into the realities revealed to us by Jesus Christ through his Word, his death, and his Resurrection. In fact, everything comes about between God, who beckons because he is love, and the human heart, which responds favorably to his invitation or rejects it. This acceptance or rejection takes place in that hidden and mysterious place St. Francis de Sales calls "the heart of the heart".

Finally, this word of advice to the retreatant: when you are making your meditations or contemplations, always have your Bible or a copy of the New Testament at hand because Jesus Christ is the only source from which the soul, as well as the Church, can draw life.

EXPLANATORY REMARKS

Read the Following Points before Beginning the Retreat

1. This retreat follows the *Spiritual Exercises*. What is the meaning of this term? It means every spiritual activity, such as the examination of conscience, meditation, contemplation, and vocal and mental prayer. Just as taking a walk, jogging, gymnastics, and swimming are bodily exercises that get the body in shape and make it more alert, so we say that spiritual exercises are every method that inclines the soul to purify itself, first from anything that puts it in disorder and distances it from God, and then renders it more aware, more determined to seek and find *what is the will of God in one's life:* in this way the "interior man" is strengthened in faith, hope, and love.

2. As a point of departure for almost every meditation a suitable Biblical text is given. This text should be read as *lectio divina,* that is, with faith and feeling, *by placing ourselves in the material place of the mystery* that is being revealed to us. These texts are generally short, and the commentary on them is brief, intended merely to be suggestive. If the retreatant relies on the simple and basic presentation of facts in the mystery and then reflects on it by himself, he may find through his own reasoning, illuminated by the Holy Spirit, something that enables him to penetrate deeper into the mystery. He will then gain more spiritual results and savor them better than if the director had explained to him the meaning of the text. *It is not so much knowledge that fills and satisfies the soul but the intimate feeling and relish of what the mystery reveals.*

3. This retreat is carried on over a period of *four weeks.* It begins, however, with a fundamental meditation: God's call to man, whom he has created. This call is a call of love, and this fact

19

should remain constantly present to the retreatant during the whole four weeks.

The First Week is devoted to meditations on the gravity of sin, which destroys the relationship of love between God and man.

The following three weeks are devoted to contemplating the life of Christ, the Word, who became man to reestablish the relationship of love between his Father and all men and, as a result of this reconciliation, a fraternal relationship between men.

The Second Week is taken up with contemplating the life of Christ our Lord up to Palm Sunday.

The Third Week is dedicated to contemplating the Passion of Christ our Lord.

In the Fourth Week the retreatant contemplates the Resurrection, the ascension, and the sending of the Holy Spirit on the apostles.

The retreat ends with the Contemplation to Attain the Love of God and to live this love in the day-to-day events of our life here on earth.

We do not mean to imply that each "week" is necessarily made up of seven or eight days. Everything depends on the amount of time it takes the retreatant to attain the interior attitude sought in each particular week. This rhythm depends on the particular temperament of and grace given to each retreatant. For example, during the First Week some may be more slow than others in coming to a repentance and sorrow for their sins. Therefore, it is necessary in each case to shorten or lengthen the week. The norm that determines the decision is whether or not the retreatant obtains the grace proper to the particular week, whatever the "state of his soul".

4. During the course of our meditation or contemplation, our interior attitude should be one of great *reverence in regard to God our Lord,* especially when we put into words whatever it is we are asking for, when we express our sentiments or desires, and when we make some act of the will, such as a resolution, choice, or decision.

5. The attitude the retreatant must have — fundamental, indis-

pensable, and unremitting—for making a good retreat is *generosity* toward our Creator and Lord. He should begin his retreat *with a great heart and totally unsparing of self*, offering to God his whole will and liberty, so that God may use who he is, and all that he has, according to his holy will.

6. It will be very helpful if the retreatant puts all of his effort into *finding what he is looking for at the particular stage of the retreat where he is* and does not busy himself considering meditations he will make in the future. Let him take each day as it comes, as if he had nothing to anticipate in the days that lie ahead. Let him be completely present to where he should be now and direct all his fervor to that topic alone.

7. The retreatant should give a full hour to each meditation or contemplation. This way he will be satisfied in knowing that he persevered in prayer during all of the allotted time. The reason for this is that, as a rule, our own apathy (and sometimes the devil) tempts us to cut short the time of prayer.

8. Mark this well: in times of fervor it takes little or no effort to spend a whole hour in contemplation, but in times of distress or boredom it is most painful to give the full time to prayer. Consequently, in order to put up a fight against this kind of desolation, the retreatant always ought to remain in the Exercise a little more than the full hour. That way he will not only get used to resisting the temptation but he will also master it.

9. If by chance we have an inordinate attachment or inclination toward something or someone, it is very good to *go against* and exercise all of our force in opposition to what we find is improperly so attractive. This way God can act with greater surety in our soul. For example, let us suppose someone is tempted to seek some kind of position, not for the honor and glory of God our Savior nor for the spiritual welfare of his neighbor but for his own interest and personal advantage. This person should make an effort to bend his desires and efforts toward the opposite, and in his prayers he should beg God not to let him want that position or

anything else unless the Divine Majesty orders his desires and regulates his first inclination to accept the position to correspond to God's will. As a result, the reasons that motivate him to take on something or to hold on to what he already has will be only the service, honor, and glory of the Divine Majesty.

10. The retreatant will make his confession to a priest of his choice. Confession is one thing; the direction of the retreatant is something else. What is important is that the director help the retreatant. For this reason the retreatant, as far as he can, should be faithful in keeping the director informed about the different moods of his soul that come as a result of his temperament or from the action of the Holy Spirit or the devil. The advantage here is that during the course of the retreat the director will be able to recommend some spiritual exercises best suited to the needs of the retreatant at the moment.

11. However little time the retreatant can give to the Exercises each day, it is essential that he *create for himself a space where there is true solitude.* If he cannot leave the house where he is living, he can at least withdraw to his room or to some other room apart from friends and from his daily occupations. This drawing himself apart has many advantages, but particularly these three:

First, because it costs him something, necessarily entailing some sacrifice, this separation from friends and occupations is of no little merit in God's eyes.

Second, because demands on the retreatant's attention coming from many quarters are reduced, he can then give his full attention to one single interest: the service of his Creator and his own spiritual progress. As a consequence, he will be more free to put to use all his faculties in seeking what he so wants to achieve.

Third, because experience proves that the more solitude and silence free the soul, the easier it is for it to approach God and wait for him. And the more our soul waits for him, the more likely it is that it will receive gifts from the Infinite Goodness of God.

12. The retreat supposes complete mutual confidence between

the retreatant and the director. If the purpose of the one is not totally clear to the other, they should discuss the matter together with simplicity and charity.

SOME SPIRITUAL EXERCISES
FOR EVERY TYPE OF CHRISTIAN LIFE

Advice on how to make
them practical and pertinent

Foreword

As we look over the set of meticulous and practical instructions that we are going to recommend to the retreatant, we should not let ourselves forget what is essential in every prayer. These instructions and these methods are merely the different paths, various ways we use to arrive at the single purpose of prayer. Each person, according to his own good pleasure, should use these means or look for others more suitable either to his temperament or to the grace he has at a particular time.

We should be convinced, however, about these two truths that are mutually dependent on each other: (1) Each one of us has his own way of praying that is strictly his own. (2) Any method of prayer (vocal or mental, ordinary or extraordinary) is not in itself better than any other type. The best method of prayer for me is determined by this particular time, these particular circumstances where I find myself. A simple "cry" toward the Lord, in the way the sick and poor of the Gospel cried, can be better for me, here, at this particular moment, than the most perfect ecstasy (Rom 8:26–27).

The purpose of prayer is to find God at the place where God wants to meet us—in our heart, as the term is used in the Bible, that is, in that secret place of ourselves that is the source of our particular personality, the place where the decisions in our lives are formed and where our destiny is hammered out. Like the high priest in the temple at Jerusalem, the only one who can enter into this "holy of holies" to converse alone with God is oneself.

Every prayer, irrespective of its form, ought to have its origin in the Word of God and its effect in a greater love of God. This is the reason why it is so important to read or call to mind a Biblical text at the beginning of the Exercise and why we must ask God for his light really to understand it and to gather fruit from it. No prayer is a good prayer unless it is made *in Spiritu Sancto:* "No one can come to me unless by the Father, who sent me" (John 6:44). The Exercise proper—meditation, contemplation, application of senses, etc.—will never be more than a deepening of the mystery spoken about in our Biblical text. The Fathers of the Church, commenting on Jacob's ladder, have already told us that every such exercise is a rung in the *Scala Christi,* the "Ladder of Christ", the summit of which is God himself.

Every Scriptural text should be approached, in all freedom, with the sole concern formulated this way by an old exegete: *"Te totum applica ad textum, rem totam applica ad te"* (Devote your whole self to the text, and its whole matter to yourself).

The sole criterion for the worth of a person's prayer is that after finishing it, he ought to live more fully the life of Christ, according to St. Paul's words: "For me to live is Christ." Are my faith, my hope, and my charity stronger after my prayer? Yes? Then all was well with my prayer, even if it was dry, distracted, or dreary.

I

COMMON FEATURES OF EVERY PRAYER
(Irrespective of What Type It Is)

Preliminary note: There are no more beautiful prayers than that one that our Savior himself taught us, namely, the Our Father, or the Angel of the Incarnation's salutation to Mary, or the everlasting canticle of heaven: Glory to the Father, and to the Son, and to the Holy Spirit.

A. How to Live in the Atmosphere of the Prayer for Each Day; This Is a Point of Capital Importance

A few practical rules to achieve this end:

— During the First Week I will not allow myself to think of things that make me feel happy or joyful, such as the glories of heaven, the Resurrection, and so forth. The reason for this is that every joyous thought prevents me from experiencing sorrow and pain for my sins. I should rather force myself to think about death and judgment.

— During the Second Week I will call to mind frequently the life of Christ our Lord, from the mysteries that I have already contemplated up to the one I am presently contemplating.

— During the Third Week I will banish joyful thoughts, even if they are good and holy. Rather I will awaken in myself thoughts of sorrow, repentance, or interior suffering by reminding myself of the burden and sufferings that Christ our Lord took on from the time of his birth down to the mystery of the Passion, in which I am at the present time involved.

— During the Fourth Week I will direct my memory and thoughts to subjects that cause me to feel happiness, pleasure, and spiritual joy, such as the glories of heaven, intimacy with God, etc.

— The bodily position I take and the physical setting of the place where I am during prayer have an influence on that prayer. So, in addition to looking at my inner dispositions, I shall pay attention to the *external behavior and circumstances* surrounding my prayer. Whether I should pray in a lighted place or in a darkened room, inside or outdoors, in a place that is cold or warm—these are factors that help some feel joyful or sorrowful; they should be used to facilitate prayer.

— During the retreat, no matter what week I am in, I will avoid anything that can distract me, and I will withdraw from conversing with others except in cases of necessity.

— Some form of *penance* will be useful, particularly in the First and Third Weeks. One should practice penance in the Second Week if the mystery he is meditating on suggests it.

— *After getting into bed at night,* just before falling asleep, I will think of the subject of my next day's meditation, and if I wake up during the night I will think about it again. In the morning when I get up and while I am dressing, I will do my best to put myself in that frame of mind that best corresponds to the mystery I am going to be meditating on soon and throughout the day.

— *Nighttime* often makes prayer easy because of its silence and solitude. But it is most important that the retreatant first take into consideration his age, temperament, and situation in making up his schedule of prayer.

— St. Ignatius foresaw that the retreatant could, if he so desired, *attend the singing of the Divine Office* when it is celebrated in a nearby church.

B. At the Beginning of Prayer

— *Before beginning prayer,* I will refresh my spirit for a moment and put myself *in a state of interior peace.* I shall do this by sitting down for a few moments or by walking around a bit (whatever seems best). During this time I will call to mind what I am about to do and why I am about to do it.

— Then I will place myself *in the presence of God:* "I will stand for the space of an Our Father, a step or two before the place where I am to meditate or contemplate, and, with my mind raised on high, consider how God our Lord watches me. Then I will make an act of reverence or humility."

— Next I will recite *the preparatory prayer.* This consists of asking God our Lord "for the grace that all my intentions, actions, and operations may be ordered purely to the service and praise of his Divine Majesty". This preparatory prayer is extremely important. It satisfies an essential requisite of every prayer, that is, a purification of thoughts and heart, a purification that in the normal course of events will gradually become perfected as the soul makes progress in the retreat.

— Following this comes *the composition of place.* Generally this is made before those contemplations or meditations that contain some potentially visible features. It consists of seeing with the eyes of the imagination or recalling the real, actual, historic, concrete place where the action of the meditation took place or where the persons I am considering lived.

Also, the composition of place can be made before a meditation whose content is purely spiritual. Then it consists of the imagination's creating a type of symbol that stands for the truth upon which I am meditating. It can also be associated with a Gospel scene. Its purpose is to create in me a "setting" for my imagination.

The use of the imagination is tricky. An image should be used in prayer only insofar as it helps us fix our interior seeing, but as soon as its purpose is realized, we should not hold on to the image. We should go beyond it in order to enter into a true contemplation.

— Finally, I will make a petition for *the grace I am looking for in the meditation.* I will ask God our Lord for "what I want and desire".

This grace varies according to the theme of the meditation or the subject of the contemplation. For example, in the contemplation on the Resurrection, I shall ask for joy with Christ because of Christ's joy; in the contemplation on the Passion, I shall ask for sorrow and compassion with Christ in the great affliction he endures.

C. During the Time of Prayer

— What posture should I take during my prayer? Sometimes kneeling, sometimes prostrate upon the floor, sometimes lying on my back, face upward, sometimes sitting down, sometimes standing, *the posture that best helps me find what I am seeking.*

— *I will remain quietly meditating upon the point (a reflection, an affective response) in which I have found what I desire* — and I will stay on at that point as long as I feel I have been satisfied.

D. Ending the Prayer

— I will complete the prayer, no matter how it has gone, with *a colloquy, a discussion,* or *a conversation.* I should reserve a long time for this colloquy. Moreover, it is all right for me to use the colloquy during the course of the meditation or contemplation as often as the Holy Spirit inspires me to do so. In fact, it is encouraged.

A colloquy means talking with God, or with the Blessed Virgin Mary, or with some saint, *exactly as one talks with another as friends do, or as a son talks with his father or his mother, or as a servant speaks with his master.* Sometimes he thanks the other for a favor, sometimes he blames himself for making a mistake, sometimes he confides with the other about his spiritual affairs, or he may ask him for advice and courage and the like. This conversation ought to be simple and informal, while ever maintaining an attitude of reverence.

— In the colloquy I ought always to speak and pray *according to the actual state of my soul.* In other words, whether I am tempted or fervent, whether I want this virtue or that, whether I want to get ready to make a particular commitment, or whether I want to be sad or joyful in the mystery I am contemplating—the point is that I should never divorce my here-and-now self from my conversation in the colloquy. The colloquy is also the time to ask again and again for what I want. A person can make one sole colloquy to Christ our Savior, but if the subject of his meditation or his own inclination calls for it, he can make three colloquies: one to our Lady, the Mother of Jesus; another to Christ our Lord; and a third to the Father.

— Every colloquy ends with *a vocal prayer.* For example, the colloquy with God our Father ends with the *Our Father,* the colloquy with Jesus with the prayer *Soul of Christ,* and the colloquy with the Blessed Virgin with the *Hail Mary.*

— It will be beneficial if, after completing the Exercise, I make a brief *review* of how the prayer went: that is, to go over the meditation or contemplation and if it was successful to thank the Lord; if it was made poorly to seek the reason why (my preparation, recollection, manner of praying). After I have found it I shall then ask pardon of God and make a firm and precise resolution concerning the cause of the failure in order to meet with success in the future.

Should I keep a journal and write down a few notes after each prayer? That depends on my preference and especially whether or not a journal is useful. If one thinks he should write down certain movements "of the Holy Spirit in his soul", there is no general direction other than that he should be guided by simplicity, moderation, and sincerity.

E. After Prayer Time

Every master of the spiritual life recommends that the morning spiritual exercise be recalled from time to time during the day, even if only for a brief moment. The reason is to enable the soul to recall how it was well ordered to God's will. And, in order to do this, these experts suggest the use of a very easy procedure which they call "ejaculations"—that is, short prayers directed toward the Lord, such as "O God, come to my aid", "Jesus, Lord", "Jesus, have mercy on me". Benedict, Bernard, Bruno, Teresa, and Francis Xavier were all in the habit of making such short prayers. Such aspirations are genuine cries of distress or of love that spring up from our very selves; they can be quite simple, yet really solid.

II

THE FRAMEWORK OF PRAYER

In this section we are going to look at the principal Methods of Prayer that St. Ignatius recommends in his *Spiritual Exercises.* These constitute a veritable education of the soul for those who want to learn to pray.

There are many methods of prayer outlined in St. Ignatius' *Spiritual Exercises.* Contrary to the legend, there is no such thing as an "Ignatian method". St. Ignatius borrowed from a number of different spiritual writers who were popular at the time what he considered to be the most teachable methods for introducing the soul to a true union with God. He made no philosophical reflections on these methods, but little by little they eventually found their way into the Exercises, and he taught his retreatants how to use them. Moreover, he realized that, once the "parameters" were mastered, the retreatant could employ them while considering the matter contained in other meditations. It is not unusual—at least when he is dealing with important topics—for St. Ignatius to ask the retreatant to apply several methods successively to the same "mystery" or even to the same "virtue" in order to penetrate more deeply into the truth of the mystery or virtue. The person who desires to unite himself with God might use one or another of these methods extensively outside the retreat, depending on his state of soul, the subject matter of his prayer, and his physical or psychological state. Furthermore, during the course of the same prayer, he might even mix these methods together. What is essential is finding God in his prayer.

We shall not here go back to commenting on the matter we have already touched on in the section entitled "Common Features of Every Prayer". We assume these topics have already been sufficiently explained for our purposes.

A. Meditation by the Three Powers of the Soul

The first time St. Ignatius introduces this method of prayer on the three powers—a method that was in vogue before his time and that was a traditional way of praying in the Church—is in connection with the Meditation on the Three Sins. Ignatius did not invent this method, and he certainly does not recommend it for anyone who finds it a detriment to prayer. Also, in the Spiritual Exercises there are many more "contemplations" than "meditations". As for the method of prayer on the three powers of the soul, the retreatant

- puts himself in the presence of God,
- makes his preparatory prayer,
- makes his composition of place,
- asks what he wants and desires.

He then uses the following procedure during the course of his meditation on a given subject or on some particular aspect of that subject.

First, he will call on his *memory.* Let us take for example the meditation on original sin. The person who sets out to consider this mystery will briefly recall to mind the story of the creation of our first parents, the gifts God gave to the first man, what he was prohibited from doing, his temptation, and finally his fall.

Second, he will focus his *understanding* on the subject. Every intellectual process that enables the person to take a better account of the theme at hand can be used: reasoning, reflection, a fortiori argumentation, comparisons, analogies, contrasts, etc. St. Ignatius uses certain phrases to identify the work of the intellect such as "to wander about the matter" or "to think over [it] in more detail". *Meditari* means "to be ruminated upon", "chewed over". St. Francis de Sales gives "understanding" the same emphasis: a person should make "one or a number of considerations" on the matter at hand.

Third, the effort on the part of the memory and understanding should *end up moving the will* or, better, *moving the heart by means of the will.* Let us note this carefully because it is what is essential in a meditation. If this factor of moving the heart is not present, the meditation will not really be a prayer. It might be a beautiful consideration, a profound reflection, but it will not be a prayer. Let us again listen to what St. Francis de Sales says on the subject. Considerations of the understanding are made "to raise your heart to God and to the things of God. This is where meditation differs from study and from considerations which are made to become learned. . . . " "As long as you are gaining light and help from any one consideration stay there without passing on. . . . " "It may happen that you find your heart raised up to God from the very beginning of your prayer, in which case there is no need to follow the method I have suggested, for though considerations usually come first, if the Holy Spirit has already brought this about they would be to no purpose."[1]

The "affections" should lead to firm, precise, sincere resolutions. To some degree the fruit of meditation is always a conversion to a more fervent love.

The meditation should end with *one or more colloquies.* These colloquies gather up all or part of what has been meditated upon. By their nature and from their results they are intimate conversations, special moments when the retreatant "applied his will to move his heart". This does not mean, however, that they are expressions of sweet sentimentality. On the contrary, they speak of a realistic commitment to God by the most sincere and total gift of self.

B. Contemplation on a Gospel Mystery

The word *contemplation* has a multifold meaning in spiritual language, and different authors give different connotations to it.

---

[1] St. Francis de Sales, *Introduction to the Devout Life,* trans. Michael Day, Cong. Orat. (Westminster, Md.: Newman Press, 1956) 57, 58, 61.

St. Ignatius defines it very precisely in his *Spiritual Exercises*. (He explains it when he treats the contemplation on the Incarnation [see p. 98].)

— After the retreatant has placed himself in the presence of God and has made his preparatory prayer, St. Ignatius asks him to *call to mind the history* (as it is described in the Bible or by one of the Evangelists) *of the mystery*. This is a most important directive because the contemplation that follows will depend to a great extent on the quality and distinctness of this recall. However, this exercise of the memory need not be a lengthy process, provided that it is precise and vivid and that it casts a spell, so to speak, on the retreatant, immersing him completely in the reality of the scene.

— Next the retreatant makes a *mental representation of the place* or the places where the mystery unfolds itself, and *then he asks for what he wants and desires.*

After this we have the following sequence:

1. The one who is praying will look at *the persons involved.*
2. He will listen to and savor *their words.*
3. He will look closely at *their actions.*

Each time, he will try to "draw spiritual profit" by reflecting on how these persons, words, and actions affect himself.

At the beginning of the Third Week, St. Ignatius introduces some new elements into the contemplation. These are, as it were, a framework of the themes that should be rediscovered during all the contemplations of that week. These themes are more allied to meditation than to contemplation:

Third Week: consider what Christ our Lord suffers in his human nature
Third Week: consider how his divinity is hidden
Fourth Week: consider how the Divinity now appears
Third Week: consider how Christ suffers all of this for my sins
Fourth Week: consider the office of consoler that Christ our Lord exercises

Ignatian contemplation consists, then, in *reliving the mystery with a great deal of faith and love;* that is, the one who is praying relives the Gospel account as if he were present there and had a part to play in the unfolding mystery. For example, at the Nativity: "I will make myself a poor unworthy slave and look upon them [Jesus, Mary, Joseph], contemplate them, and serve them in their needs, as though I were there present, with all possible homage and reverence." Contemplation also requires some of the elements of reflection and meditation. In this sense it is distinct from that method called "Application of the Senses".

Like meditation, contemplation should terminate with the colloquies, where affections intermingle with resolutions.

C. Application of the Senses

St. Ignatius explains this method in connection with the Meditation on Hell (see pp. 78–81).

— After placing himself in God's presence, saying the preparatory prayer, calling to mind the history of the mystery, making the composition of place, and asking for the grace he wants, the retreatant is ready to employ this method. It consists of *exploring the mystery, so to speak, with the aid of each of the five senses.*

First with seeing: The one making the prayer *sees* with the imagination the persons who are involved in his Exercise, and he meditates and contemplates in detail on the circumstances in which they find themselves. Then after what he has seen, he endeavors to draw spiritual profit by reflecting *on himself.*

Next with hearing: The person making the prayer *hears* what the persons say or what they could be saying. As a result of what he hears, he endeavors to draw spiritual profit by reflecting *on himself.*

Then with smelling and tasting: For example, at the Nativity: "To smell and taste with the interior senses of smell and taste the infinite fragrance and sweet savor of the Divinity, of the soul and of its virtues, and of all else, according to the person we are contemplating . . . " Then, to reflect *on oneself* to draw profit from this contemplation.

— The application of the senses also terminates with *colloquies,* where affections of the heart and resolutions of the will are intermingled.

This method is closely connected with contemplation, but it penetrates even more deeply into our feelings and is, so to speak, more refined and intuitive. St. Ignatius uses it frequently, either for subjects that of their very nature are moving (for example, hell) or at the end of the day so as to impress upon the retreatant even more thoroughly a scene upon which he has already made a number of exercises (for example, the birth of our Lord) or when the meditation is one that seems to him to be of exceptional importance (for example, the Two Standards). In these last examples, the Application of the Senses is already a part of the important method of "repetition".

This process of getting a hold on spiritual realities through the five senses is part of the intuitive order. It grasps these realities by a single flash of insight, which is possible only when there is a simplification of spiritual activities. It greatly outstrips the slow and somewhat heavy march of meditation by the three powers of the soul, and it even surpasses the analyses of contemplation. However, it presupposes both. It takes place at the end of the day so that the fruit of the preceding exercises can be gathered and savored.

D. Repetition of One or Many Exercises

Repetition enjoys a very important role in the Exercises conducted over a period of thirty days (it is hardly possible for us to make use of it on a regular basis in this *Do-It-at-Home Retreat*). St. Ignatius envisaged the retreatant's making four and sometimes five exercises during a single day — and sometimes even on the same topic.

If, however, the retreatant who follows the schema contained in this book wishes to make use of the repetitions, let him do so with complete freedom.

Whatever the retreatant decides, it is essential that he know something about this excellent method of meditation. It is through the repetitions that the soul steeps itself more and more in the mystery or the truth upon which it has been meditating. Each person has his favorite mysteries from the Gospels and the particular words of Christ he savors most. For him there is a grace connected with scenes of these particular mysteries, something that "sings in him" when he contemplates them. It is most profitable, therefore, to return to them frequently in perfect freedom.

The repetition begins the same way as all of the Exercises: with the placing of oneself in the presence of God, the preparatory prayer, the history of the mystery, the composition of the place, and the asking for grace.

After this, the retreatant repeats the preceding exercise or exercises. But he does so with this important difference: he says, *"I will return to where I dwelt upon those points in which I experienced greater consolation or desolation or light or greater spiritual appreciation."* In addition to giving this advice, St. Ignatius also recommends developing "colloquies", which are important in the development of these points, for it is the heart that always forges ahead in meditating on a particular Gospel event.

It is not a question, therefore, of merely repeating our consideration of ideas or reflections. What is essential is the *spiritual experience* we had during our meditation, and now what we want to do is relive those motions within our soul, those times when God was experienced in clearer way. In short, we want to return to the "warmest", the most effective, and most meaningful points in those meditations we have already made.

It should be noted that St. Ignatius includes "desolations" among these experiences that he asks the retreatant to go back and relive. We will only draw attention to the importance of this piece of advice without giving it a long treatment here. But at least we should remark that, in Ignatian spirituality, confrontations with what pains the soul are precious indeed because they are the "nights" when faith is made more pure, hope more ardent, and love more sincere.

There are times when St. Ignatius seems to envisage a type of repetition that is more objective and seems to be more like a resumé. "The intellect, without distractions, will turn over assiduously the remembrance of the matter contemplated in the preceding exercises." So what was contemplated the first time is made more real, is better integrated, and becomes more internalized. It is even possible that, due to this "perseverance", God's will for the retreatant will become manifest to him.

III

THREE METHODS OF PRAYER

A. Prayer That Evolves from Our Daily Living

St. Ignatius' First Method of Prayer is actually *a method that engages ourselves and our daily lives in a very concrete and realistic type of praying.* Rather than a "method" properly so called, it is a form of exercise designed to stimulate the soul to make progress in virtue, while at the same time it brings to life a prayer that is pleasing to God. It is, if you like, a method for revising one's life, for *revitalizing one's prayer life.*

The person who wishes to pray according to this method should begin with one of the following: God's Ten Commandments, the seven capital sins, the powers of the soul, or the five senses of the body.

He should observe all of the exercises prior to beginning the actual prayer: selecting a time when he can withdraw from acquaintances and occupations, placing himself in God's presence, and making the preparatory prayer. If, for example, he is going to use the Ten Commandments, his preparatory prayer should include petitions asking God our Lord to show him how up until now he has failed to live the Commandments, begging God for the grace and help to enable him to make amends in the future and for a perfect understanding of these precepts so that he may observe them better for the greater glory and praise of his Divine Majesty.

1. *The Commandments*

I will consider and reflect upon the first commandment: How have I observed it? How have I failed to observe it? As for the length of this consideration, I will give it about the time it takes me to say three Our Fathers and three Hail Marys. If during this time I discover I have failed in any way, I will ask pardon and forgiveness for my faults, and I will say an Our Father.

Note: Obviously, if this reflection leads me to conclude that I am not in the habit of sinning against a particular Commandment, I will not spend a long time considering it. But if I discover there is a Commandment I trip up on from time to time, I will devote a longer period of time to considering and examining it. This same rule pertains to the subject of the following section, the capital sins.

After I have gone through the Commandments in this way, accused myself of my faults, and asked for grace and help to amend my life in the future, I will end the prayer with a conversation with God our Lord.

2. *The Capital Sins*

The same procedure that is used for the commandments should be followed as far as the capital sins are concerned. The only difference is that I should avoid dwelling on what goes into making the sin sinful. Rather, I should consider the virtues opposite to these vices in order better to realize the faults I have committed regarding the capital sins.

3. *The Powers of the Human Soul: Intellect, Imagination, Will*

The same recommendations given in connection with the Ten Commandments should be followed in respect to the three powers of the soul.

4. *The Five Senses of the Body*

Here again the same method should be followed.

The person who wants to imitate Christ our Lord in the use of his senses will recommend himself to his Divine Majesty in the preparatory prayer. Then, after he goes through examining himself on each sense, he will say one Hail Mary and one Our Father.

If he wishes to imitate our Lady in the use of his senses, he will recommend himself to her in the preparatory prayer, asking that she obtain from her Son and Lord the grace he needs for this purpose. Then, after an examination on each of the senses, he will say one Hail Mary.

B. Prayer That Evolves from Spoken Words

This is a method that is extremely simple and practical. St. Ignatius and St. Francis Xavier taught it to people who were beginners at prayer, and they also recommended it to those who were advanced in the spiritual life, even those favored with extraordinary graces in prayer.

A person making this type of prayer will withdraw from friends, acquaintances, and worldly cares to pray in secret.

The preparatory prayer will vary according to the person to whom the prayer is made.

This *Second Method of Prayer* consists of the following: I will either kneel or sit, taking any position where I find I am more comfortable in prayer and where I obtain greater devotion. Then, either closing my eyes or fixing them on some point from which I do not allow them to roam, I will say the words "Our Father". I will consider these words for as long as I find new meanings, comparisons, pleasure, and spiritual joy.

Then I will do the same for each word in the prayer Our Father.

I can use this same method with any other prayer or canticle that I particularly like.

The primary rule to be observed in this method of prayer is that when a person finds in one or two words a great deal of matter to reflect upon, as well as much consolation and fervor, he should not be concerned about going on to another set of words, even if he remains on one or two words during the whole time allowed for this prayer.

At the end of the fixed time, it will be good to finish by saying the whole prayer over briefly in the ordinary way, leaving for another day a consideration of the words remaining. The retreatant should also make a colloquy to the person to whom the prayer is addressed, asking in a few words for the virtues and graces that he feels he has more need of at that given moment. Finally, according to however he feels, he can say a few other vocal prayers.

C. A Rhythmic Prayer

In preparation for this prayer the retreatant should observe the recommendations to stop what he is doing and pull himself away from friends and acquaintances to make his prayer.

The preparatory prayer will vary according to the person to whom the prayer is addressed.

The *Third Method of Prayer* consists of measuring my prayer in accordance with my breathing. For instance, at each breath I will say one of the words in the Our Father (or any other prayer), and while saying the word I will pray mentally. I will do so in such a way that during each interval that separates one word from another I will try to deepen in myself the meaning of the word or consider the person to whom I am addressing my prayer, or I will endeavor to reflect on my own condition.

Every person should feel free to combine vocal prayers with this measured, rhythmic prayer and to apply this type of prayer to a number of prayers he might say during the course of his meditation. The essential thing is to unite himself with God.

We should point out here the relationship of this type of prayer with the well-known prayer in the East called the *Jesus prayer.* The basic principle is "to have Jesus enter the heart" (heart in the Biblical sense, that is, the primary source of all of a man's life and activities). The Jesus prayer consists of repeating slowly and indistinctly, in rhythm with the inhaling and exhaling of air—that is, in rhythm with the breath of life itself—this Gospel-like invocation in which one can easily recognize the prayer of the man born blind and the prayer of the publican: "Lord Jesus, Son of God, have mercy on me, a sinner." This simple formula contains the whole mystery of Christian life: living with the resurrected Jesus Christ. It can be simplified even more. At its peak, the Jesus prayer consists in merely repeating the name "Jesus" and finally in the simple awareness of his presence in the deepest part of one's heart.

There are other *methods of prayer*. Some of these have even come from non-Christian religions, for example, Zen and yoga. No method of prayer should be disdained. It is up to each person to choose the type that best suits his temperament and the grace he has received. What is essential is that one be recollected and find the living, personal, "good" God within himself, "at the heart of his heart", so that faith, hope, and charity will expand in him.

Today, rather than concerning ourselves with methods, we would rather deal with that with which every prayer should be concerned: alienation, loneliness, the intimate realization of the needs of the Church and of the world, the knowledge of the Word of God, etc. But we should remember that one category does not exclude consideration of the other!

IV

METHOD FOR THE DAILY EXAMINATION OF CONSCIENCE

A. The General Examination of Conscience

There are five steps in this method. Ordinarily it is made once a day, in the evening.

First point. I will thank God our Lord for the graces, both spiritual and temporal, that I have received, particularly for those received since my last examination of conscience.

Second point. I will ask for the grace to know my sins and to struggle to rid myself of them.

Third point. I will review my conduct, hour by hour, or period by period, from the moment I woke up in the morning until the time of making this examination. I shall examine first of all my thoughts, then my words, then my actions, or I will use some other formula that may be better suited to me.

Fourth point. I will sincerely ask pardon from God our Lord for the faults I have committed.

Fifth point. I will make the resolution to amend my life with God's grace. In order to make this amendment I will try to foresee the difficulties that lie ahead from the time of this examination to the next, and I will ask God our Lord to enlighten me and come to my help when I face them.

I will end my examen the same way I end my meditations, that is, with an Our Father.

Important note: this type of examination of conscience takes about fifteen minutes, but the five steps are more important than the duration of the examen itself. To devote the whole fifteen minutes to thanking God might be a good prayer, but it would not be an examen. If I spend but a few minutes on the final steps of the examen, my examen might be hasty and superficial, but it would still be an examen.

B. The Particular Daily Examen: Three Different Times and Two Examens Involved in This Practice

First time. In the morning, immediately after getting up, I ought to resolve to be on the alert during the whole day to guard against the particular sin or fault that I seek to overcome or remedy.

Second time. Either before or after lunch, I will ask the Lord for what I want, namely, the grace to be aware of all the times I have fallen into that particular sin or defect and the grace to correct it and to make amends.

Then I will make my first particular examen. Here I examine myself with regard to the particular sin or fault I have resolved to get rid of. I shall do this by passing in review each hour or the various projects that have filled my schedule since the time of my rising until the moment of my present examination of conscience.

If it is helpful, I will register in some kind of notebook the number of my failures. This practice might enable me to keep a daily or weekly record of the results of my endeavors.

Finally, I will renew my resolution to struggle against this sin or particular fault during the second half of the day.

Third time. Either after dinner or just before going to bed, I will make the second examen in the same way I made my first. As before, I shall go over each hour that has passed, but now it will concern the time from my afternoon examen until the present time.

Important notes:

1. The purpose of the particular daily examen need not be restricted to correcting defects. It can also be used to help acquire some particular virtue and to put it into practice.

2. During the retreat a person can use the particular examen to remove the faults and negligences with regard to his fidelity in following the directives pertaining to the Exercises.

Is It Good to Make a General Confession during or after the First Week of the Exercises?

There is no obligation in this matter. Each one should feel free. Making a retreat is one thing; going to confession is another.

However, the person who spontaneously decides to make a general confession will find many advantages in doing so, among which are these three:

1. There is more profit and merit attached to making a general confession than in making an ordinary confession because of the greater sorrow one feels for his sins and for all the evil in his whole life.

2. During the time when one is making the Spiritual Exercises, he has far more personal insight into his sins and their perversity than at any other time. Moreover, as a result of this awareness and sorrow, he will draw from his confession greater spiritual profit and merit than he would draw at another time.

3. As a result of his making a better confession and being better disposed, he will be more prepared to receive the Holy Eucharist. Communion not only helps one avoid sin but also constantly increases grace in us.

If the person chooses to make a general confession, it is best to do so immediately after finishing the exercises of the First Week. (*See no. 10 in "Explanatory Remarks" on p. 22.*)

PENANCE

Penance can be either interior or exterior.

Interior penance consists of having sorrow for our sins with the firm purpose of not commiting them, or any sin, again. This is not an intermittent sentiment but one that is constant, and it forms part of a Christian's normal state of soul, just as sin forms part of our lives.

Exterior penance is the result of interior penance and consists of inflicting punishment on oneself for the sins that he has committed.

Exterior penance can be divided into two categories: involuntary and voluntary.

The chief type of exterior penance, if one can really call it penance, is involuntary. This consists of a filial acceptance of everything that constitutes our human condition, such as work, suffering, and death; and everything that makes us die bit by bit, such as age, sicknesses and infirmities, reverses of fortune, aches and pains, separations from and mourning of loved ones, etc. We should never forget all the consequences and punishment due to sin (*"Morte morieris..."*: "If you disobey me", the Lord said to man, "you will die the death..."). Let us accept it just as it is.

To this first and chief type of involuntary penance is added exterior penance that is voluntary or freely imposed.

Exterior voluntary penance is practiced in three ways:

1. The first method is concerned with *food*. When we put aside whatever is not essential in regard to eating, we practice, not penance, but rather temperance. Penance comes about when we abstain from eating what is normal for us to eat. The more we do

without it, the greater is the penance; however, we must watch out that we do not compromise our health.

2. The second method deals with *sleep.* Here also there is no penance when we give up what is unnecessary and what causes us to be soft and lazy. There is penance when we reduce the amount of sleep that is normal and natural to us. And, provided our health is not harmed, the more we reduce it, the better is the penance. In case one has the habit of sleeping too much, he should cut back on his normal amount of sleep for a short time in order to come to a happy mean.

3. The third method consists of *chastising the body,* or in other words in inflicting physical pain on it. This is done by the use of penitential instruments: whipping cords, hairshirts, little chains made of metal. In this type of penance, it is proper to use only those instruments that cause superficial and external pain and do not result in leaving bruises. *Note: It is of vital importance that a person who feels, either within the retreat or outside it, that he would like to use penitential instruments should put himself under the direction of a prudent director and abide by his advice in this matter.*

Let us add here two remarks:

1. Voluntary exterior penances aim at accomplishing three principal effects: first of all, to make satisfaction for past faults; next, to conquer oneself—that is to say, to order our sensible nature so that it will obey our conscience; finally, to seek and obtain a grace that we earnestly desire—for example, deep sorrow for sin or compassion for the pains and sufferings that Christ our Lord endured during his Passion or perhaps for light needed to clarify some question that we are wrestling with. For these reasons exterior penances are closely linked with the prayer of petition.

2. When the retreatant does not achieve what he desires during the course of the Exercises—for example, the feeling of contrition for his sins—it is often a good idea for him to make some changes in the way he eats, sleeps, or practices penance. Therefore, for two

or three days he should practice some penance and then for two or three days not perform any at all. It is a fact that the spiritual advantages of penances vary with each individual. Another fact is that we often stop doing penance because of our sensuality or because of an inordinate concern for our health. But it can also happen that a person can put too many demands on his body by exaggerating his penances. God our Lord knows our human nature infinitely better than we do, and so in this matter of penances we must experiment in order to find what is proper for each individual.

NOTE TWO

THE SPIRITUAL EXERCISES
AND THE MYSTICAL LIFE

All of the commentators of the *Spiritual Exercises* have noted that St. Ignatius speaks only of the purgative way (First Week) and the illuminative way (Second, Third, and Fourth Weeks and the Tenth Annotation of the *Exercises*) but never of the unitive way. We believe this omission is deliberate and that in Ignatius' thinking it corresponds to a certain concept of what the unitive or mystical life is. We will deal with this subject in this note.

We will limit our investigation to what is contained in the methods of prayer, meditation, contemplation, application of senses, repetitions, and the three types of prayer.

None of these methods by itself presumes that a person has been called to go beyond the normal operations of the soul or that he has received exceptional graces of prayer. On the contrary, all of them seem to suppose that the person normally has to make an effort to recollect and to prepare himself for prayer, to fight off distractions, and the like. In short, each one of these methods supposes that the soul manages itself, with God's grace, rather than being acted upon and taken over directly by God.

Having established this fact, we would now like to emphasize that it is more than clear that God can unite himself to a person through any of these methods, even when the person makes a simple vocal prayer, and God can do this in an unexpected and exceptional way. Without stipulating active or passive states of prayer or specifying normal or extraordinary kinds of prayer, St. Ignatius very prudently speaks to us about such topics as savoring, spiritual quiet, meditation, contemplation, and the like. He was by no means ignorant that each one of these states of the soul has hundreds of nuances and degrees, depending upon the person making the exercise and the particular moment when that exercise is made. As far as he is concerned (and this goes for the director of a retreat as well), Ignatius prefers to focus on the movements of the Holy Spirit within the person's soul, movements that he calls consolations (fervor, joy, enthusiasm) and desolations (sadness, turmoil of spirit); and he knows that in the last analysis the only spiritual harvest that counts is an increase of faith, hope, and charity and a growth of divine life within the soul.

A person "succeeds" in making the Spiritual Exercises if, during the course of each of the weeks, he passes through these states of the soul wherein his soul "wants and desires" and asks God for grace to realize his desires. It is these states of the soul that guide the person in forging a more and more secure union of his soul with Christ our Lord.

One very typical example of St. Ignatius' concept of the "mystical" can be found in what he says about "tears" during the First and Third Weeks. He actually has us asking God for the gift of tears. Does he consider that these are the sure sign of repentance and spiritual grief that the remembrance of our past sins and the contemplation of Christ's Passion ought to stir up in us? Does he consider tears a normal grace or an exceptional grace? It would seem that there is no satisfactory answer to such questions—and there are many more like these—that would apply to every person at all times. Tears, like contrition and interior joy, can be a natural reaction to feelings, but they can also be a "sudden and unexplained" grace from God or the result of an activity that combines the human and the divine. The director's role is to help the retreatant steer clear of illusions and search in his encounters with God for perfect sincerity and honesty. There is always one test that never fails, however, in determining the authenticity of all mystical phenomena, and that is this: Do the mystical phenomena bring on an increase of faith, hope, and charity? If so, they are good. If not, they are vain occurrences, and at times they can even greatly harm the soul.[1]

[1] St. Francis de Sales gives an enlightening interpretation of St. Ignatius' thinking on this point. In his treatment of "spiritual raptures", he distinguishes between ecstasy of the intellect, ecstasy of the will, and "ecstasy of activity, of life". The first two, he says, are liable to illusions and even to pride. Only the third, which manifests itself in daily self-renunciation and submission to the will of God, is reliable and is the measuring stick for the other two. It alone causes us to die to ourselves and "live in God with Jesus Christ". Are not we then able to say with St. Paul: "The life I live now is not my own; Christ is living in me" (Gal 2:20)? This attitude alone is the criterion for living in accord with genuine love. (Cf. bk. 7, chap. 6 in St. Francis de Sales, *The Love of God: A Treatise,* trans. and introduced by Vincent Kerns [Westminster, Md.: Newman Press, 1962], 286–89.)

THE SPIRITUAL EXERCISES

To Build My Life
on God's Love,
That Is to Say, to Order My Life
and to Direct It
Solely According to God's Plan
for Me

There are two types of retreats:

    — retreats during which one makes a choice of a state of life,

    — retreats during which one reforms a state of life already chosen.

In both cases the structure of meditations is the same.

MAN WAS CREATED TO LOVE GOD

*That Is to Praise, Glorify, and Serve Him and by
These Means to Achieve His Eternal Destiny
(This is the primary and fundamental aspect of my life.)*

I exist . . .

What is the origin of this existence? Its meaning? Its worth? This is the capital question that I should ask myself as a human being.

The Bible, particularly the New Testament, answers it for me this way:

1. Man was created by God in his image and likeness. Genesis 1:26–27: "God said, 'Let us make man in our own image, in the likeness of ourselves.'"

"Because God is love" (1 John 4:16): man therefore is made to love with his heart, which is like God's.

2. God created man to love him with all his heart, all his mind, and all his strength.

Deuteronomy 6:4–9: "'Hear, O Israel! The Lord is our God, the Lord alone! Therefore, you shall love the Lord, your God, with all your heart, with all your soul, with all your strength. Take to heart these words that I enjoin on you today. Drill them into your children. Speak of them at home and abroad, whether you are busy or at rest. Bind them at your wrist as a sign and let them be as a pendant on your forehead. Write them on the doorposts of your houses and on your gates.'"

Man loves God first of all through praise, adoration, and service. It is along these lines that I should *order,* that is, regulate, all of my existence.

3. But love means more than this. Love of its very nature seeks union. God created man out of nothing to make him God's adoptive son in Jesus Christ and by Jesus Christ.

God's plan therefore consists in enabling us to participate here on earth (by faith and grace) and for all eternity (in a more intimate friendship) in the life of the Trinity.

"My dear people," St. John writes (1 John 3:2–3), "we are already the children of God, but what we are to be in the future has not yet been revealed; all we know is that when it is revealed we shall be like him because we shall see him as he really is."

At the Last Supper, after his farewell discourse and priestly prayer (John 13:31–17:26), it is Jesus himself who shows us the meaning of our existence in all of its magnificence. Let us relish words such as: "On that day you will understand that I am in my Father and you in me and I in you.... If anyone loves me he will keep my word, and my Father will love him and come to him and make our home with him" (John 14:19, 23). "I have given them the glory you gave to me, that they may be one as we are one. With me in them and you in me, may they be so completely one" (John 17:21).

We can deepen our appreciation of God's "hidden plan he so kindly made in Christ" for us by reading the first three chapters of St. Paul's letter to the Ephesians: everything comes from God's love; everything should be returned to God in love.

4. I learn the answers to these questions through Jesus' response to the lawyer who asked him: "Master what must I do to inherit eternal life?" (Luke 10:25), or from the scribe who asked him, "Master, which is the greatest commandment of the law?" (Matt 23:34–40; Mark 12:28–34). He said, "You must love the Lord your God with all your heart, with all your soul, and with all your mind. This is the greatest and first commandment. The second

resembles it: You must love your neighbor as yourself. On these two commandments hang the whole law, and the prophets also." And, according to Luke, Jesus said, "Do this and life is yours" (Luke 10:28).

At the end of these reflections it would be well to pray on the Our Father, the Magnificat, or simply on our "Act of Charity" according to the second or third method of prayer.

THIS FUNDAMENTAL TRUTH
REGULATES MY RELATIONS
WITH OTHER MEN

And, in General, with All Beings
That Enter into My Life. It Also Governs My Attitude
in Respect to All Situations and Events
in Which I Find Myself Involved

1. I do not exist alone on this earth. There are other creatures, too—money, food, plants, animals. There are various conditions of body and soul: wealth and poverty, good health and bad, sadness and joy, success and failure, honors and humiliations. There are the circumstances of my state of life, my family life. And most especially, there are other men who have the same divine destiny as myself.

It is necessary that I set up a network of ordered relationships with everything that is "created": ordered according to God's order, ordered according to the absolute, exclusive nature of his plan of love: "You worry about so many things, and yet few are needed, indeed only one" (Luke 10:42).

All created things wait for me to give them a meaning. For "the whole of creation is waiting with eagerness for the children of God to be revealed . . . with the intention that the whole creation itself might be freed from its slavery to corruption and brought into the same glorious freedom as the children of God" (Rom 8:19–21).

2. Here then is the rule that imposes itself on me: *all things on*

the face of the earth are created for man to help him to achieve his destiny as a son of God.

From this it follows that man should make use of created things insofar as they help him in the attainment of his destiny and that he should have nothing to do with them insofar as they are an obstacle or hindrance to him.

In other words, I ought to love everything with the heart of a son, that is, according as God, my Father, wants each thing for me. And I ought to rid myself of them with the heart of a son, according as God, my Father, does not want them for me.

3. God manifests his will to me by his Providence as Creator (ordinarily he desires that man be healthy in mind and body, that families be united, that justice and love reign between men [see the Commandments, the counsels, the Beatitudes]). He does so through the teachings of his Son Jesus Christ and through what happens to me. His "order" is not a static, unchangeable order; it is a living order, revealing itself to me day in and day out, in the changing circumstances of my life; it is a dynamic order in which light and strength are together progressively revealed in my human conscience.

4. Because at each instant, I conduct myself as a son of God in respect to every single "created thing", *it is necessary that I remain indifferent to all created things as far as I am allowed free choice and as far as God does not prohibit me from choosing them. Consequently, for my part I do not will health more than sickness, riches more than poverty, honor more than dishonor, a long life rather than a short life, and so for all other things, but I will desire and choose only those things that lead me to the end for which I was created, that is, to love God.*

5. This fundamental *indifference* is a difficult yet critical way of looking at things. It must be understood in the light of the Gospel: to be indifferent means placing the love of God before every other love and every other aversion. It is living out charity.

Indifference is a free and deliberate choice: "I choose God . . . and with his grace, I shall always be faithful to this choice."

— Indifference, therefore, does not mean being unconcerned or insensitive: I can have a horror of sickness and death and yet love them because they are God's will for me, etc.

— Indifference does not take away those things I spontaneously find attractive or repulsive because of my personality or temperament, but I "accept" them only insofar as they concur with God's will for me. Indifference is a disposition of my freedom that makes no choice before knowing that God wants that which I choose.

— A "passion" ordered to God would be good; one that was inordinate or not disposed to his will would be evil. So it is a matter of "orienting" our temperament, our "heart" in a radical way. Compare the outbursts of anger and tenderness of a St. Paul: grace does not do away with these, but it directs them in terms of the love of Christ.

— Far from putting a damper on my enthusiasm for the projects of my personal, familial, professional, or social life, indifference really stimulates them: it is God's will that "I am" and that I strive toward being, for myself, for others, and for the world more of what I am. At the same time, however, when the will of God is that I fail, that I become less important, or that I die, indifference enables me to accept failure, setback, death as a mysterious success: Did Christ save the world more by his work in Nazareth or his miracles and preaching than by his Passion?

— The type of the perfectly indifferent man was the one God called in the Bible *"my just one"* and *"the man after my heart"*, that is, Abraham, Job.

6. To sum up: *indifference* does not mean anything more than this profound, living disposition of spirit that enables me to choose this attitude freely with God's help: "God is everything for me; apart from him whatever is created is nothing. *Todo . . . nada.*"

My desire is to turn resolutely toward God and whatever God wants me to love.

Pray over these reflections

— while going over slowly the Act of Charity,

— while making acts of offering—"I desire and choose God . . . I desire and choose whatever will draw me closer to God"—like the baptismal promises,

— while repeating: "Our Father . . . thy will be done on earth as it is in heaven".

FIRST WEEK

Sin shatters God's plan of love.
The sinner no longer lives with God
in a relation of son to Father.

If I am in the state of sin,
in order for me to return to the love of God I must
honestly recognize my faults,
be moved by confusion and repentance,
sincerely ask pardon for them
from my Father in heaven and from the Church,
and relying on God's help
I must turn toward a better future.

If I have already been pardoned
or if I have remained faithful to my baptismal promises,
it is essential that I recognize,
according to St. Paul's expression, that
"what I am now
I am through the grace of God" (1 Cor 15:10).

The First Week is the week of humility and generosity,
the week of necessary purifications.
Its purpose is to create in me an attitude that ought to be
a permanent feature of my spiritual life.

THIRD DAY

WE MUST SEE SIN THROUGH GOD'S EYES, NOT THE EYES OF THE WORLD

Put yourself in the presence of God and make the preparatory prayer. Ask him to inspire you.

Composition of Place

I will cast myself in the role of one of these three individuals; I will assume their sentiments and make them my own:

— The tax collector in Luke 18:13, who "stood some distance away . . . not daring even to raise his eyes to heaven".

— The prodigal son in Luke 15:18, who said, "Here I am dying of hunger! I will leave this place and go to my Father."

— The good thief at Calvary in Luke 23:41: "In our case we deserved [the sentence we were given]."

I will ask God our Lord for what I want and desire. Here I will ask to see clearly in what way I have sinned and to feel the gravity of sin as it is described in the Gospel so that I may be sorry and ashamed of myself if I have committed sin often. And I will ask to be grateful, humble, and vigilant if the Lord has kept me until now in my baptismal innocence.

First Point: The Fall of Lucifer and His Angels

My *memory* will remind me what the Bible and the Church teach: created in the state of grace, Lucifer and his angels revolted against

God. Their fault was a *fault of pride*. They then went from the state of grace to the state of sin. They were separated from God, cursed by God. This is hell.

Next I will apply my *understanding* to this subject. I shall assess the weight of original sin, which misrepresents every perfection, however beautiful it is (the idea of the Pharisee). I will become aware of the need of recognizing God as the author of every good and of every virtue. I will call to mind the disastrous effects resulting from one sole mortal sin either in the visible world (the account of Judas) or in the invisible world (the Mystical Body), and in contrast, I shall recall the good that has come from one act of God's love (the conversion of St. Paul; Mary's Yes at the Annunciation, etc.).

My *will*, aided by faith, will penetrate as deeply as possible into the core of the mystery of sin (particularly the sin of pride), to appreciate its ingratitude, its "folly" toward God the Father. Either vocally or mentally, and with all the sincerity I can muster, I will make acts of repentance, of a firm purpose of amendment, of gratitude, of humility.

Second Point: Man's Sin

My *memory* will conjure up for me the Genesis account of sin in terms of its spiritual message: the creation of man and woman in original justice, the confidence God bestowed upon them when he put them over all creatures and invited them to collaborate with him in his completion of creation, God's prohibition, the woman's and man's disobedience in order to "be like gods", the loss of original grace, and the entrance of sin into the world. Hence God's plan seemed thwarted.

My *understanding* will reflect on these Biblical facts. It will weigh sin not with human scales (a passing and hardly serious human act) but with divine scales (the relationship with God broken, creation altered, the human conscience wounded, the sufferings and death of Jesus Christ on the Cross to make reparation for sin, the reestablishment of order, the reconciliation with the Father and the restoration of peace, charity among men).

My *will,* placing itself resolutely on the level of faith, will adhere with all its strength to what God has revealed to us in the Bible about the gravity of sin, about the redemption, about his compassion for the repentant sinner. In imitation of the Blessed Virgin Mary it will offer itself to participate energetically with Christ in the great work of the redemption of the world, in the restoration of justice everywhere in this world.

Third Point: The Sin of Someone Condemned to Hell

We must beware of putting a name on any particular person who is "damned". Who knows God's secrets? And his mercy? We proceed no further than to say that Jesus clearly acknowledged the existence of hell.

We simply remind ourselves of certain words found in Scripture, for example, these severe warnings: "Causes of falling are sure to come, but alas for the one through whom they occur! It would be better for him to be thrown into the sea with a millstone around his neck" (Luke 17:1). "And if your hand should be your downfall, cut it off; it is better for you to enter into life crippled than to have two hands and go to hell . . . where the fire will never be put out" (Mark 9:43–48).

I will make use of my *understanding* in my effort to penetrate the meaning of these words. Thus, for example: the Lord of goodness and compassion has revealed these realities to poor men like myself who are weak and tempted. Sin therefore is something that is serious—one of the most serious matters I have to consider. It is my everlasting life or death that is at stake.

I will become aware of the weakness of my *will* without God there to sustain it, without his strength. As a consequence of this realization I shall make not only acts of repentance and humility but also acts of confidence and abandonment. Jesus said, "Cut off from me you can do nothing" (John 15:5), and St. Paul, "I am a creature of flesh and blood sold as a slave to sin. I do not understand my own behavior. I do not act as I mean to, but I do things that I hate" (Rom. 7:14–15).

Prayer in the Form of a Conversation with Christ

Imagining Christ our Lord before me nailed to the Cross, I will speak with him, asking him how it is that though he is the Creator, he has become man; and how it is that he came from eternal life to die such a death for my sins at a particular time.

Then, *looking into myself,* I will ask

— What have I done for Christ?

— What will I do for Christ?

— What ought I to do for Christ?

Finally, in seeing him in this plight, nailed to the Cross, I will ponder over whatever presents itself to my mind.

I will finish the meditation by reciting the Our Father.

Note: This colloquy, provided that it is extremely personalized, is one of the most important in the Spiritual Exercises. It pertains to my life here and now, not my past. It is in my present state that I should "order" the way I shall act tomorrow. Each person has his history; each one has his destiny. It is this existential ensemble of past and future that the retreatant ought to ponder before Christ accomplishing his destiny on the Cross.

LOOKING AT MY PERSONAL SINS

Put yourself in the presence of God and make the preparatory prayer. Ask him to inspire you.

Composition of Place

This can be the same as for the preceding exercise. I will ask for *what I want and desire.* Here it will be sincere repentance and genuine sorrow for my sins.

First Point: The Review of My Sins

I will call to mind all the sins of my life, reviewing my life year by year or period by period. The following classifications will help me in this consideration:

1. where I have lived,
2. my dealings with others,
3. what responsibilities I have had; my calling in life.

We should avoid, however, drawing up a juridical, meticulous inventory, and even more we should watch out for any type of scrupulosity. This review should be done in the light of the Holy Spirit; that is to say, it should be done in an atmosphere of adoration, gratitude, and a deep appreciation of a grace-filled life.

Second Point: I Will Weigh My Sins and the Gravity of Their Disorder

Every capital sin—and to a certain extent any sin—is in itself a transgression against man's conscience and very often an offense against others. This is so even if God did not expressly forbid it. Sin, then, is a disorder in my own personal life and in my dealings with others.

Third Point: I Will Honestly Consider Who I Am before God

Who am I? (1) What am I compared to all men? (2) What are men compared with all the angels and saints? (3) What are all the angels and saints compared with God?

Then, just myself, what am I before God?

So it is this weak, finite being who stands up against God and says, "I will not serve. I will not obey." There is something in common with Satan's revolt at the core of every sin.

Being aware of what my sins are *in reality*—even those that at the time seemed to me to be of little consequence but to which I fully consented—makes me conclude that I have preferred myself to God.

Fourth Point: I Will Turn toward God and Say to Him:

Who are you, Lord? Who are you?

And I will in this way compare his wisdom with my ignorance, his power with my weakness, his justice with my iniquity, his goodness with my wickedness, his love with my selfishness, etc. The gravity of sin and the pains of hell are understood properly only when we contrast them with "the extraordinary love with which God has loved us".

Fifth Point: Profound Wonder but Also Immense Gratitude Now Overwhelm Me

The Lord spared me at the time of my sin. Creation did not rise up against me but remained subdued, supportive, while I was saying "no" to the Creator. God's work of creation continued on for me and for my enjoyment. Had I really been aware of this patience of his, "a cry", in St. Ignatius' words, "of wonder accompanied by surging emotion" would have escaped my lips. And then there is St. Bruno's aspiration: "Oh, pure goodness!"

I will conclude my meditation by addressing a prayer first to our Lady. I will ask her to obtain for me three graces from her Son: (1) the grace to see my sin with his eyes and to detest it as he detests it; (2) the grace to feel, even to the point of experiencing shame, an abhorrence for the disorder of what is sinful in my life so that I can put it in order; (3) the grace to discern what is good and what is evil in the world so that detesting what is evil I can put it away from me. I will then say a Hail Mary.

Afterward I will make the same petitions to Jesus, asking that he obtain from his Father these graces for me. Then I will say some prayer such as the Body of Christ.

Finally, I will address the Father, asking that he, the Lord eternal, grant me these three graces. Then I will say an Our Father.

FIFTH DAY

COLLOQUY OF MERCY

We have already noted on pages 40–42 that the repetition is a most effective Exercise. We shall use it here. After the examination of conscience we made yesterday, it will be good today to go back and consider that magnificent colloquy of mercy that ended our meditation of the Third Day.

Put yourself in the presence of God and make the preparatory prayer. Ask him to inspire you.

Composition of Place

"Imagine Christ our Lord present before you nailed to the Cross . . . seeing him in this plight, nailed to the Cross."

Let us look closely at our crucifix: we stand before him with the burden of our personal sins and also, because we are members of the Church, with the weight of the sins of the world.

I will ask for *what I want and desire:*

— in the light of the Cross of Christ better to understand interiorly the mystery of sin,

— to see and understand sin as God sees and understands it, not as the world judges it.

First Point: "Asking Him How It Is That though He Is the Creator, He Has Become Man"

Indeed, this is a mystery. To appreciate it, we must ask God himself. He alone can respond.

Let us slowly read the passage where St. Paul expresses his astonishment and admiration in Philippians 2:6–7: Jesus Christ, "being in the form of God, did not count equality with God something to be grasped at. But he emptied himself, taking the form of a slave, becoming as human beings are."

This is the first step of the Son of God's self-abasement.

Indeed, the Word of God's way of proceeding is exactly the opposite of the way a sinner operates.

— Revolt is the motivation for the sinner. For Christ it is selflessness and obedience.

— For the sinner it is pride. For Christ it is stripping himself of his divine prerogatives; it is humility and even embracing humiliations.

With him how far we are from any type of love that is conditional, calculated!

Verbum caro.... The Word was made flesh ... Adore....

What a refinement of human nature!

"You will be like gods", Satan said to the man and woman, and they sinned.

And now that has been realized, and even more than realized: man, in uniting himself with the Word Made Flesh, becomes a son of God, is "one" with God.

Second Point: "How Is It That He Has Passed from Eternal Life to Death Here in Time?"

This is the second cause of astonishment, the mystery that is even more bewildering than the Incarnation: he who is presented to us as Life everlasting ("I am the Life", "I am the Resurrection and the Life") knows death in time, death on the Cross.

In the passage from Philippians cited above, St. Paul describes Christ's death on the Cross as the final step in all his actions of self-abasement: "And being in every way like a human being, he was humbler yet, even being obedient unto death, death on a cross" (Phil 2:7–8).

Indeed, this death of God on a cross is a stumbling block and folly for men. As St. Paul wrote: "We are preaching a crucified Christ: to the Jews an obstacle they cannot get over, to the gentiles foolishness, but to those who have been called . . . a Christ who is both the power of God and the wisdom of God" (1 Cor 1:23).

Before, death had been an obstacle and a scandal to human intelligence, but how much more of an obstacle and scandal is it when it includes him who said that he was "Life Everlasting"? Only the Resurrection could solve—up to a point—this problem and could resolve this apparent contradiction.

And yet Jesus Christ went even as far as that.

Third Point: The Only Response to These Two "How Is It That's?"

Only one answer: "God is love" (1 John 4:8).

"God so loved the world that he sent his only son" (John 3:16).

"Love consists in this: it is not we who loved God, but God loved us and sent his Son to expiate our sins" (1 John 4:10).

But if so much love was necessary to make amends for our sins, then sin is a grave matter, infinitely grave. Is it not true that on the moral and spiritual plane it is the most grave matter there is?

Indeed. For it ruins "the purpose and good pleasure" that God had determined for man from all eternity. It would take the Passion and death of God to reintroduce us into the intimacy of the Trinity.

*Fourth Point: "Then I Will Reflect upon Myself and Ask: 'What Have
I Done for Christ? What Am I Doing for Christ? What Ought I to
Do for Christ?'"*

I will look at myself now as I am at the present moment. What is
the connection between me now and what I have been meditating
on? I should see my life only in the light of the love with which I
am loved. The law of love is exacting. St. Ignatius remarked: "It is
good to call attention to two points: the first is that love ought to
manifest itself in deeds rather than in words." The second is that
"love consists in a mutual sharing of goods."

1. "What have I done for Christ?" More of a confusion and
shame about myself and about the niggardliness and lukewarmness
of my love than about my sins, which I should not bother to
enumerate.

2. "What am I doing for Christ?" The mediocrity of my life.
My defects. My lack of purpose and courage.

3. "What ought I to do for Christ?" A firm purpose. An ideal
in life that goes beyond the firm purpose. St. Paul's message to the
Colossians maps out for us the way to love: "I make up for what is
lacking in the sufferings of Christ for the sake of his body, the
Church" (Col 1:24).

Let us note "for Christ", a phrase that is repeated over again
like a refrain. We are not face to face with a code, a law, but with
Someone who loves us and who calls us to love in return:
"Everything in Christianity", Claudel said, "always comes down
to a face-to-face encounter."

I will end this meditation (which is merely a long dialogue
with Christ) with a most intimate Our Father, which I will recite
very slowly. God's plan for man and for creation is contained in its
entirety in this prayer, "which our Savior has taught us".

SIXTH DAY

HELL EXISTS: JESUS CHRIST
HAS ATTESTED TO THIS FACT
BY HIS WORD AND HIS DEATH

Following the grace we have received up until now and our own preference, we will meditate today on the account of the prodigal son (Luke 15:11–32), or on the woman who was a sinner in Simon the Pharisee's house (Luke 7:36–50), or on Peter's denial (Mark 14:66–74), or, even better yet, on hell. Some of the saints have revealed to us what kind of a role the fear of God's judgment—a salutary, filial fear based on faith—has played in forming their attitudes and in their sanctification.

This prayer on hell will introduce us to a new method of prayer, one that is called the Application of the Senses (see p. 39).

This prayer demands a great spiritual simplicity on the part of the retreatant, a kind of special skill that will enable him to hear Jesus' words just as he said them and as the people of Galilee understood them.

But first we call to mind two pieces of advice from St. Ignatius and one important spiritual principle:

1. "It is not much knowledge that fills and satisfies the soul, but the *intimate understanding* and *relish* of the truth."

2. "*I will remain quietly* meditating on the point in which I have found what I desire, without any eagerness to go on until I have been satisfied."

And our spiritual principal: the Application of the Senses is built up in stages from the most materialistic (the senses of the body) to the highest spiritual prayers (the senses of the soul).

Depending on what appeals to him and on the grace he has been given, each person picks out what he wants from along this whole scale.

Put yourself in the presence of God and make the preparatory prayer. Ask him for his grace.

Composition of Place

One of the following:

— before Michelangelo's well-known fresco "The Last Judgment" in the Sistine Chapel,

— before some medieval tympanum or stained-glass window depicting hell,

— the scene of the Last Judgment described in Matthew 25:31–46.

I will ask *for what I desire and want:* here it will be a deep sense of the pain that the lost suffer, so that if I ever forget the love of my Father in heaven, at least the fear of these punishments will keep me from falling into sin. (We should not forget that each time he spoke of hell, our Lord presented it with an almost brutal realism. Our prayer ought to preserve our Lord's same "tone of speaking".)

First Point: To See with My Eyes

1. What the Gospel calls the "darkness outside":

"But the children of the Kingdom will be thrown out into the darkness outside" (Matt 8:12).

"As for the good-for-nothing servant, throw him into the darkness outside" (Matt 25:30).

St. John and St. Paul present the redemption as a battle between Light and Darkness. I will strive to enter into that vision of the world.

The Passion is presented as the hour of the "power of darkness". I will see the darkness that covered the earth at the moment of Christ's death (Luke 23:44 and Matt 27:45).

2. The "fire": *"In ignem aeternum . . . "* Compare the great scenes of the Last Judgment (Mark 13; Matt 24) and also Matthew 18 and Mark 9.

"It is better for you to enter into life with one hand, one foot, one eye than . . . be thrown into the hell of unextinguishable fire."

Second Point: To Hear with My Ears

1. The "cries" of the damned (Matt 8:12; 24:51; Luke 13:28),

2. Their "grinding of teeth"; *stridor dentium* cited twelve times in the Gospels,

3. In the parable of Lazarus, the appeals the rich man made in his conversation with Abraham (Luke 16:19–30),

4. The terrible sentences meted out to the damned at the Last Judgment ("Go away from me, with your curse upon you" [Matt 25:41]).

Third Point: To Smell the Odor

This is the "corruption" of which St. Paul speaks (Gal 7:8; 1 Cor 9:25; 15:53) and about which St. Peter writes (1 Pet 1:23).

Fourth Point: To Taste

Such bitter things as tears, sadness, remorse of conscience:

— the thirst of the evil rich man in his torment (Luke 16:24)

— the bitterness of divine wrath, the despair of the damned, the "second death" in comparison to the "life" of love and joy the

Word incarnate came to announce and promise in the name of his Father

Fifth Point: To Feel by My Sense of Touch

1. The "rejected" at the Last Judgment . . . like the bad fish the fisherman rejects; like the chaff they separate from the good grain and burn; like the dinner guest at the feast who was without the proper garment; a force that pushes us to the outside; a brutal, definitive decision with no appeal,

2. The fiery furnace: "the fiery lake of burning sulphur" (Rev 19:20; 20:10),

3. Contacts with the damned, the demons . . . what surroundings! We who were made to be "one" with the Trinity, to live eternally in the company of the Virgin Mary, the angels, and the saints.

I will enter into conversation with our Lord. I will call to mind those who are in hell. Some did not believe in his coming; others who did believe nevertheless did not keep his commandments, of which "the first and the greatest" is "you shall love . . ." I will then thank him that he has not let me die at those times when I was unfaithful, that he came to find me in my wretchedness, and that he has always and unceasingly treated me with so much tenderness and compassion.

I will close my prayer with an Our Father.

SEVENTH DAY

WHAT IS DEATH FOR THE CHRISTIAN?
IT IS TRUE LIFE

It is fitting that we should end this first week with a vision of faith and hope. Despite sin, God's plan can be realized, is realized. The most cruel affliction of sin remains: "You shall most surely die" (Gen 2:17), but henceforth death is changed: for the elect it is a passage, the passage to life everlasting in heaven.

Place yourself in the presence of God and make the preparatory prayer. Ask him to inspire you.

Composition of Place

Calvary at the moment of Jesus's death . . . or before Lazarus' tomb when Jesus called him forth.

I will ask for *what I desire and want.* Here it will be that my faith in eternal life will be firm and profound and that from this moment forth I be one of those to whom the marvelous promise of St. Peter pertains: "God called you out of darkness into his wonderful light!" (1 Pet 2:9).

First Point: The Mystery of Life and the Mystery of Death

1. Life is a mystery, but we have some experience of it. Because we have no experience of death, it is even more of a mystery. Without Christ's revelation it is the "black hole". Death is "absurd" and makes life also "absurd".

2. And yet death is life's most certain fact. I will die. But this certain fact is wrapped up in uncertainties. St. Francis de Sales says this about it: "One day, my soul, you must depart from this body. When will it be? In winter or summer? In town or country? During the day or night? With or without warning? As a result of illness or accident? Shall I have a chance to go to confession? . . . Unhappily, I know none of these things; only one thing is certain: I will die, and sooner than I imagine."[1]

Second Point: Death Is the Great Separation

And for this reason it is the great light of truth.

1. At the instant of my death the world dies *for me*. It is all over. It topples over into nothingness *for me*.

2. No. Not everything is finished. At that same moment, God sorts the weeds from good grain that grew up during my soul's time on earth. It is the moment of truth: there is that which remains and lives on because it was built upon God, and there is that which dies and disappears because it was "handed over to vanity". Please God there is nothing in me that merits this "second death" about which St. John speaks in his book of Revelation (Rev 20:14).

3. Seen in this light everything during a person's earthly life that "mortifies" (that is, puts to death) takes on its true worth. "In my estimation all that we suffer in the present time is nothing in comparison with the glory that is destined to be disclosed in us" (Rom 8:18). In this light we understand better what St. Paul meant when he wrote to the Corinthians: "Yes, the troubles that are soon over, though they weigh little, train us for the carrying of a weight of eternal glory that is out of all proportion to them" (2 Cor 4:17). On condition that "the troubles" are joined to the Passion of our Lord: "Because you have died through your baptism, and now the life you have is hidden with Christ in God.

---

[1] St. Francis de Sales, *Introduction to the Devout Life*, 30–31.

But when Christ is revealed—and he is your life—you too will be revealed in all your glory with him" (Col 3:3–4).

Third Point: Death for the Christian Is a Passage to Life

We should relish the words in the First Preface of the Mass for the Dead with all the savor of faith and hope these words contain: "Lord, for your faithful people life is changed, not ended" (it goes from the temporal to the eternal). This wonderful metamorphosis— the grain of wheat that dying gives birth to the shoot or the chrysalis that becomes a butterfly—gives us some idea, however imperfect, of this process.

1. Life everlasting—this is what Jesus, the Word made flesh, has come to bring us here below. By his death and Resurrection he has conquered death, the result and the symbol of sin. "Death, where is your victory? Death, where is your sting?" (1 Cor 15:55). Jesus presents himself to men as the Life, the Bread of Life. Let us reread St. John's magnificent sixth chapter or the account of the raising to life of Lazarus (John 11).

2. Life everlasting is heaven. Heaven is God possessed, loved for all eternity; better, it is God possessing us, loving us, uniting us to himself during all eternity. Let us reread chapter 21 in the book of Revelation, or the Second Letter to the Corinthians (5:1–10), or many a chapter from the New Testament. Our basic, existential appetite for life, for joy, for love, for unity will be altogether satisfied, fulfilled. Death enables the faithful Christian to pass to this unhoped-for state of being "face to face" with God. "Now we see only reflections in a mirror, mere riddles, but then we shall be seeing face to face" (1 Cor 13:12). "My dear friends, we are already God's children, but what we shall be in the future has not been revealed" (1 John 3:2).

3. Far from making us "hate" the world, this perspective should incite us to save the world, as far as it is in our power to do so, to work for its sanctification and for man's progress toward unity

and charity. Let us not forget that "the whole of creation, until this time, has been groaning in labor pains" (Rom 8:22). We achieve our own personal salvation in the perspective of "knitting God's holy people together in Christ" (Eph 4:13). "But our homeland is in heaven, and it is from there that we are expecting a Savior, the Lord Jesus Christ, who will transfigure this wretched body of ours into the mold of his glorious body, through the working of the power that he has, even to bring all things under his mastery" (Phil 3:20).

SECOND WEEK

Jesus Christ,
God made man,
embarks on the redemption of the world.

He restores God's plan of love.
He reconciles men with his Father
and man with his fellow man.

With his light and through his grace
he invites me
to take my personal place
within the life of the Trinity
and, as a consequence,
within the world of men.

THE CALL OF CHRIST, OUR LEADER

*Contemplated through the Symbolic Call
of an Earthly King*

1. This juncture in the Exercises poses a very serious problem for us: Who should go beyond this point to make the three remaining weeks? In the Eighteenth Annotation St. Ignatius writes: "If the director sees that the retreatant has little aptitude or little natural ability, that he is one from whom little fruit is expected ... let him go no further to take up matters of election on the choice of the way of life and any other exercises that are outside the First Week." This ability to proceed further is a gift, but it should be understood as the ability of a person to live the spiritual life in the fervor and generosity of love. Never did St. Ignatius exclude from the Christian elite the humble, the uneducated, or the poor of spirit. His experience was like that of St. Francis de Sales, who confessed: "I have found God full of sweetness and perfume among the highest and hardiest mountains, where many simple souls cherish him and adore him in complete truth and sincerity." So we should read in St. Ignatius' wise recommendation nothing more than that every retreat should be adapted to the temperament and the grace of the retreatant.

2. In Christian life there are not two faiths, two hopes, and two charities (see Eph 4:5). All the baptized have the vocation to be "perfect as [their] heavenly Father is perfect" (Matt 5:48). But there are hundreds of degrees of generosity, hundreds of ways to distinguish oneself in his service, and these differences depend on temperament and grace.

3. The image of the temporal king—an image borrowed from the chivalry of Ignatius' time—may cause problems for some

people today. If such is the case, they should recall the image some of the Jews had about the Messiah at the time of Christ, that is, that he should be a military leader, God's Chosen One who would restore the kingdom of Israel and lead her people to victory and to the conquest of the world. If the Biblical image of a military leader shocks some, then these people might substitute for it a political figure, or an inspired thinker, a great reformer, or an academic leader.

Place yourself in the presence of God and make the prayer beginning the meditation considering how God watches you. Then make the act of reverence and humility.

Ask him to inspire you and help you.

Composition of Place

This will be to see with the imagination the synagogues, villages, and towns where Christ our Lord preached.

I will ask for *what I want and desire.* Here it will be for the grace not to be deaf to the Lord's call but to be prompt and diligent to accomplish his most holy will.

IN THE FIRST PART, LET US CONTEMPLATE THE CALL OF AN OUTSTANDING KING, CHOSEN BY GOD

First point. I will imagine an earthly king *chosen by God our Lord himself,* to whom all Christian princes and people pay respect and obedience.

He is therefore a leader who enjoys the prestige of having been the one chosen out of all Christendom by God himself, an extraordinary chief whose program and whose promises are wonderful.

Second point. I will consider how this king speaks to all his own: "My will is to conquer all the lands of the infidels. Therefore, whoever would wish to come *with me* must be content with the *same* food *as I,* the *same* drink, the *same* clothing, etc. He must also labor *with me* by day and watch *with me* by night, etc., so that he can share *with me* in victory just as he has shared *with me* in suffering."

The conditions for being a companion of the king are therefore most exacting and demanding. Accepting companionship with him implies a "co-sharing" with him in the strictest sense of the term. That is, it covers all of the circumstances and every moment of one's whole life. It means partaking of his toil and sufferings as well as of his victory, which from this moment on has been guaranteed.

Third point. I will consider what type of an answer his faithful subjects will give a king who is so generous and so compelling. If anyone refused the invitation from such a king, he would deserve to be reprimanded and considered fainthearted.

Here we are introduced to an extremely important feature in the spiritual teaching of St. Ignatius, his appeal to the "heart" of a person, to his noblemindedness, his affinity for deep, intimate friendship, generosity, enthusiasm. We are reminded here of the advice we gave the retreatant before beginning the Exercises, namely, that his primary disposition for receiving gifts and favors from God should be generosity, offering his entire will and liberty to God so that he may dispose of him, make use of him, according to his will.

THE SECOND PART OF THE EXERCISE CONSISTS IN APPLYING THE EXAMPLE OF THIS KING TO CHRIST OUR LORD

First Point: Facts and Reality

The whole scope of this contemplation is in St. Ignatius' question: "How much more . . . ?" and then his invitation to the retreatant to draw the inferred conclusion.

If an invitation of an earthly king to his subjects is so wonderful, *how much more* is it worthy of consideration that we look at Christ our Lord, *the eternal King,* who invites the whole universe and at the same time *each person in particular* to come before him. To these he says, "It is my will to conquer the whole universe and all my enemies and thus to enter into the glory of my Father. Therefore, whoever wishes to come *with me* should labor *with me,* so that in following me in suffering *he may follow me* also in glory."

We are in a setting that is right out of the Gospels:

1. Jesus is the eternal King.

2. His call is made to the heart of each person. "Follow me." "If anyone wants to be a follower of mine, let him renounce himself and take up his cross and follow me" (Matt 16:24; Mark 8:34). "No one who does not carry his cross and come after me can be my disciple" (Luke 14:27).

3. His purpose is to "recapitulate" in himself the whole universe, visible and invisible. In the text of the Ephesians upon which we have already meditated, St. Paul writes: "[God the Father] has let us know the mystery of his purpose, the hidden plan he so kindly made in Christ from the beginning to act upon when the times had run their course to the end: that he would bring everything together under Christ as head, everything in the heavens and everything on earth" (Eph 1:9–10).

4. Moreover, the victory in Christ's battle is already certain: "I have conquered the world", he says at the hour of his Passion (see John 16:33).

Second Point: The First Response

I will consider that all those who have sound judgment will offer themselves unreservedly for this task.

Very important: the invitation is the same to all; the difference comes in the responses. Christ our Lord invites all men: "Be perfect, as your heavenly Father is perfect" (Matt 5:48). Each one responds to this call according to his grace, in the mystery of his personal fidelity.

This first response is already very lofty. It is total, without reserve. Everything is accepted. But between this response and that of the *insignes,* that is, those who "distinguish or signalize" themselves, there is a distance that separates the love that comes from making a choice from reasonable motivations, including even personal interests, and a pure, unselfish love that is willing to take risks in the unconditional gift of self.

We will meet the two types of responses again (the response of reasonable people and that of the *insignes*) during the course of the Second Week, the week of "choices".

Third Point: The Response of the Insignes

These make the same response as those who are reasonable, but they make it differently. They make it with their whole heart.

Those who shall be more desirous to show affection and signalize themselves in entire service of their King and Lord of all will not only offer themselves entirely for the work but, more, will also act against their selfishness and against all worldly love and make offerings of greater value and more importance, saying:

> Eternal Lord of all things, I make my offering with your favor and help, before your Infinite Goodness and before your glorious Mother and all the saints of your heavenly court; I want and desire, and this is my deliberate choice, provided that it is only for your greater service and praise, to imitate you in bearing all injustices and contempt, and all poverty, both real and spiritual, if your Most Holy Majesty wishes to choose and admit me into this state of life.

We should carefully note that in this offering there is no question of religious life, or of religious poverty, but of the evangelical poverty of the Christian.

It is possible that we would falter before making such an offering. Some might then advise us to ask God at least for the desire to desire to make such an offering. But it would be better to say: consider to what extent Christ has loved you. "[He] loved me and gave himself for me" (Gal 2:20). And then, relying on his grace, agree to go wherever he would like you to go. Say with St. Paul: *"Scio cui credidi"* (I know in whom I have put my trust) (2 Tim 1:12).[1]

Important note: It is obvious that this contemplation is connected with everything Jesus Christ has revealed to us about the "Kingdom of God" and the "Kingdom of heaven" and, as a consequence, with everything that touches on preaching the Gospel in the world and with the mission of the Church here on earth. This is a meditation that is far-reaching and very difficult because the distinction between "temporal" and "spiritual" is complex, yet this distinction is of paramount importance. Reread, for example, the bewildering dialogue between Jesus and Pilate: " 'So, then you are a king?' Jesus answered, 'It is you who say that I am a king. I was born for this; I came into the world for this: to bear witness to the truth" (John 18:37; cf. 19:13–16, 19–23). Then recall that the apostles found it difficult indeed to free themselves from the image of a military Messiah in charge of a temporal kingdom (Acts 1:6–9). Then there is the example of Paul, who had no hesitation about taking his images out of a military armory: "Put on the full armor of God. . . . And you must take on salvation as your helmet and the sword of the Spirit, that is, the Word of God" (Eph 6:10–17).

[1] Beginning with the Second Week and during the rest of the retreat it will be most profitable to spend some time reading the Bible (especially the New Testament) or some life of a saint. The important thing is to choose these readings to complement the spirit of the meditations of the particular week in the Exercises where one finds oneself.

THE "WITH ME" IN CHRIST'S CALL
AS SEEN FROM ST. PAUL'S PERSPECTIVE

What are the elements that go into making up the mystical life of a Christian? St. Paul gives the complete answer to this question when he writes to the Galatians (2:20): "I have been crucified with Christ, and yet I am alive; yet it is no longer I, but Christ living in me."

The mystical life is essentially "being united" with Jesus Christ and through him with the Father. It consists of growth in grace, and grace is simply God's life, the divine life in us. The mystical life of a Christian is therefore a growth in faith, hope, and charity. Here on earth the culmination of this life is the martyr, the one who dies with Jesus Christ to live with Jesus Christ.

Consequently this life consists of entering into the mystery of Jesus in order to die with him so that I can be raised up with him. This is the life of the "new creature" that here on earth we live through faith and hope and that after our death we shall live in the full light of the vision of glory.

In order to express this reality of our Christian life, of living out this unity with Christ in life and in death, St. Paul has created a whole vocabulary of verbs that begin with the prefix *sun* in Greek (*cum* in Latin), that is, "with". A meditation on the Call of the King from St. Paul's point of view will enable us to see his call and also his Kingdom in their various spiritual dimensions.

Place yourself in the presence of God and say the prayer to begin the meditation.
Ask him to inspire you.

Composition of Place

Either Jesus' speaking with Nicodemus on the need for man's being "reborn" (John 3:4) or on Calvary at the time when the centurion's lance pierces Jesus' side (John 19:43).

I will ask for *what I want and desire.* Here, I will ask not to be deaf to the call of the eternal King but to be prompt and diligent to accomplish his most holy will.

First Point: Baptism: "Plunged" into Jesus' Death in Order to Be Raised up with Jesus

It is baptism (and the act of faith that it supposes) that transforms us with Jesus Christ into sons of God.

Romans 6:2–11: "Are you not aware that we who were baptized into Christ Jesus were baptized into his death? Through baptism into his death we were buried *with him* so that, just as Christ was raised from the dead by the glory of the Father, we too might live a new life." In verse 5 St. Paul insists: "If we have been united *with Christ* [*complantati*] through likeness to his death, so shall we be through a like resurrection."

What is the life of Christ? After our baptism, what is our life? "His life is a life for God. In the same way, you must consider yourselves dead to sin but alive for God in Christ Jesus."

Second Point: "In novitate vitae": In a New Life

The effect of baptism is immediate. Our spiritual resurrection is not the same as the resurrection to come. It is a resurrection in faith, one that has taken place here and now.

As of now we are the "resurrected".

What does this mean?

1. It means we are "dead to sin" and that as a result we must, with Christ, fight against all of his "enemies", that is, against our concupiscence and selfishness: "Our old self was crucified with Christ to the Cross" (Rom 6:6). "God has rescued us from the

power of darkness and brought us into the kingdom of his beloved Son. Through him we have redemption, the forgiveness of our sins" (Col 1:13–14).

"All of you who have been baptized into Christ have clothed yourselves with him" (Gal 3:27).

The result of this is that we go beyond "co-sharing with Christ" in his work to a veritable unity in Christ. In order to express this marvelous and mysterious reality, St. Paul created a formula that has no equivalent anywhere in the Greek language: *En Christô,* that is, *in Christ.*

2. What we have become, in Jesus Christ the Son of God, and what we will be in the future are explained to us by St. Paul in his Epistle to the Romans (8:16–17): "You have received a spirit of adoption through which we cry out, 'Abba' [Father]. The Spirit himself gives witness with our spirit that we are children of God. But if we are children, we are heirs as well: heirs of God, heirs *with Christ,* if only we suffer *with him* so as to be glorified *with him.*" The Holy Spirit is the great craftsman in creating our unity with Christ, and he does so just as he unites the Father and the Word in the Trinity.

3. The three theological virtues accompany divine grace in us:

Faith, which enables us to live the invisible and makes the invisible present, real, to us.

Hope, which enables us to possess the invisible now.

Charity, which unites us with the invisible.

These virtues reach their fullness according to how the Christian lives out his baptismal grace and how he progresses in becoming united with Christ. They always remain the "rock" upon which his total Christian life is built.

Third Point: Progress in Unity with Christ

As long as we are on this earth, this "new life", which we receive in baptism and in our initial act of faith, should expand and grow.

1. This growth always takes place with Christ, in terms of the regular fluctuation of death and resurrection, as it appears:

a. Through the sacramental life, particularly in the Eucharist.

b. By our acceptance of our human condition, that is, our death and everything that prefigures that death in us. It is the deepening of St. Paul's statement: "In my own flesh I fill up what is lacking in the sufferings of Christ for the sake of his body, the Church" (Col 1:14).

c. Through all that we do on both the purely human and the spiritual levels. It is through our activities that we are engaged here on earth in the very same combat in which Christ was involved.

d. Through our life of serious prayer. By our contemplation and through the mediation of love, our prayer becomes divine life within us: "The Spirit too helps us in our weakness, for we do not know how to pray as we ought; but the Spirit himself makes intercession for us with groanings that cannot be expressed in speech" (Rom 8:26).

2. Through an intensification and a purification of faith, hope, and charity within us. We can come to appreciate the usefulness of "nights", whatever their origin—from the spirit or the senses— because they strip away from us everything that is nonessential, and they force us to center ourselves on God alone.

3. Everything in our lives that appears to us, either from close range or from afar, to be associated with the witness of the martyr (trials, persecutions, religious vows) is of the greatest worth in uniting us with Christ, of "plunging" us into the mystery of his death and Resurrection.

Fourth Point: It Is in Heaven Where the Full Maturation of This Grace Is Realized. There We, Who Have Suffered with Jesus Christ, Will Be Victorious with Him

1. There is only a flimsy veil between grace and glory. If, as St. John says, "we are God's children now, what we shall be later has not come to light . . . when it comes to light we shall be *like* him, for we shall see him as he is" (I John 3:2); then, between grace and glory there is only "*a twinkling of an eye* [*ictus oculi*]" (I Cor 15:52).

2. Yet, from now on, this "new life" must be seen as reality, and our eyes must see all things as God sees them: "New heavens and a new earth" (Rev 21), because for the person who lives in faith, hope, and charity, heaven is already here on earth.

I will carry on a conversation with Jesus Christ in which I will renew my offering of service in the Kingdom to him. And I will listen to him say to me: "*Dilexi te* . . . I love you, and I have delivered myself for you."

I will also talk over all of this with the Blessed Virgin Mary, asking her that I may "be placed with Jesus Christ" (St. Ignatius summed up in this formula his whole notion of sanctity), and I will ask her to teach me to be content to be "the companion of Jesus", to be "one" with him. "This alone is enough for me", as the dying St. Bernadette said, clasping her crucifix.

I will conclude with the Our Father and the Hail Mary.

TENTH DAY

THE MYSTERY OF THE INCARNATION

Place yourself in the presence of God and make the preparatory prayer. Ask him to help you.

I will call to mind the *history* of the subject that I will contemplate. Here it will be from St. Paul's Epistle to the Galatians (4:3–6): "In the same way, while we were not yet of age we were like slaves subordinated to the elements of the world; but when the designated time had come, God sent forth his Son born of a woman, born under the law, to deliver from the law those who were subjected to it, so that we might receive our status as adopted sons." This contemplation will then unfold like a triptych with three panels side by side. In the first panel we see the three Divine Persons, how they are looking down on the whole expanse of the world filled with men who live under the slavery of sin. In the central panel we see them determining from their eternity to send the Second Person to become man to save the human race. Finally, in the third panel we see that when the fullness of time arrives, they send the Angel Gabriel to our Lady. At each point of my contemplation I will return to these three scenes of the triptych.

Let us now follow up on the realities that these Biblical scenes represent and on the particular historic event that is taking place.

Composition of Place

Here I will see the great extent of the earth's surface, where so many people of so many diversified backgrounds have lived in the past, are living in the present, and will live in the future.

Especially I will consider the house and room of our Lady at Nazareth in Galilee, seeing it as a place of light amid so much darkness and shadows.

I will ask for *what I want and desire.* Here it will be an interior knowledge of the Lord, who is made man for me so that I may love him more and follow him more closely.

First Point: I Will Look at the Persons Depicted in These Scenes

1. The various people throughout the world. I will see them in their great variety of dress and ways of living, where they are, and what kind of civilizations they have: some are white, others black; some are at peace, others at war; some are weeping, others laughing; some are in good health, others sick; some are being born, others dying.

We have here the same theme of contrasts and the same kind of description as we find in Ecclesiastes 3:2–9: "A time to be born and a time to die." All of this is quite existential. The stress is on a real awareness of the human condition in its diversity and its contrasts.

This pagan world is a world of slavery, rivalries, war, hate. Except for a few people of goodwill, or the "just" who have remained upright, it is a world that never witnesses an act of the love of God or hears a cry of fraternal charity.

2. I will see and consider the three Divine Persons, enthroned in their majesty. They look upon the whole world and all the people who are living in such blindness and corruption. What has become of the people whom they created "in their own image and likeness"? In what a state do they live and die!

3. I will look at Mary at prayer in her room at Nazareth, and I will consider the angel greeting her. *Full of grace,* full of love for God, full of love for men.

I will reflect on these scenes and draw spiritual profit from them.

Second Point: I Shall Listen to the Words Spoken

1. What are the people saying? What does their speech mean as they converse with one another? How many lies, examples of false witness, errors, etc.? How often do they speak to God or against God? Let us reflect for a moment on the "news" diffused today throughout the world by the press and all types of mass media.

2. What are the three Persons saying? Eternal words! Just as one day they said, "Let us make man in our own image, after our likeness" (Gen 1:26), today they say, "Let us redeem the human race."

And I will reflect on what St. John said: "Yes, God so loved the world that he gave his only Son" (3:16). "God's love was revealed in our midst in this way: he sent his only Son to the world that we might have life through him" (1 John 4:9).

Also what St. Paul wrote to the Ephesians (1:4): "God chose us in him [our Lord Jesus Christ] before the world began, to be holy and blameless in his sight, to be full of love ... through Christ Jesus to be his adopted sons." The unique and eternal Word of God!

3. Reread the Gospel account of the remarkable conversation between the Virgin Mary and the Angel Gabriel at the Annunciation (Luke 1:26–38).

I will reflect on all I hear to draw spiritual profit from these words.

Third Point: I Will Look Closely at the Actions of the Persons Depicted in These Scenes

Actions reveal what is in the heart; they disclose our deepest feelings, and they measure the amount of our love.

1. The men on the face of the earth. How far are we from the new commandment: "Love one another!" The world is an extended

battlefield where each person looks out for his own interests, every one of which is determined by his ambition, passions, and covetous desires.

2. The Father who "sends" his Son. His Son replies, "I am here, Father, to do your will!" The Father pardons men; the Son offers himself and delivers himself to them. The divine "mission" is thereby begun—a mission that, after the death, Resurrection, and ascension of Jesus, will be carried out by the Holy Spirit until the end of the world.

3. The *"Verbum caro factum est"* (the Word was made flesh) is fulfilled in Mary. Let us adore in silence.

Let us give the full sense, the real, and the very concrete sense to this *"caro factum est"*, as St. Paul does: "His Son, who was descended from David according to the flesh" (Rom 1:3) . . . "from them [our fathers] came the Messiah (I speak of his human origins)" (Rom 9:5).

This realism is very important for the accuracy of our religious thinking on this subject of the Incarnation. We must eliminate from such terms as the Eucharist, the Cross, the Resurrection, and the Divine Motherhood anything that smacks of the hazy or the fuzzy. We are dealing here with Reality, a Reality even more real than that grasped by our senses.

Even in his time St. John bewailed the false teachings regarding the Incarnation: "Many deceitful men have gone out into the world, men who do not acknowledge Jesus Christ as coming in the flesh" (2 John 7).

I will look at our Lady as she humbles herself and gives thanks to the Divine Majesty.

I will then draw spiritual profit from the considerations on this point.

Finally, I will *converse* with the three Divine Persons, with the eternal Word incarnate, and with the Virgin Mary, asking them, according to inspirations I now feel within me, to help me in every way to follow more closely and imitate better our Lord, who has just now become man "for me": "He loved me, and he became incarnate for me."

I will end my contemplation with an Our Father, and with the angel at the Annunciation I shall repeat the Hail Mary.

ELEVENTH DAY

CHRIST'S BIRTH AT BETHLEHEM

Place yourself in the presence of God and make the customary prayer at the beginning of the contemplation.
  Ask him to inspire you.

I will call to mind the history of the mystery: our Lady, about nine months pregnant, and Joseph set out from Nazareth in Galilee to Bethlehem, the city of David, in Judea, to enroll in the census that the Emperor Augustus had recently ordered and to pay the tribute that the Emperor had imposed on all the lands conquered by Rome.

Composition of Place

Here I will see in my imagination the road going from Nazareth to Bethlehem: its length, breadth, the foothills it goes through . . . I will also see the cave at Nazareth, the manger where the Savior was born; his hardships; his needs; how Mary and Joseph are attending to everything in a spirit of poverty.

  I will ask for *what I want and desire.* Here it will be to know our Savior who has become man for me so that I may love him more and follow him better.

First Point: I Will Look at the Persons

Our Lady and St. Joseph; then, after he is born, Jesus. I will make myself a poor or lowly, unworthy servant. I will watch them,

103

contemplate them, and serve them in their needs, just as if I were present, with all the devotion and respect possible.

Then I will reflect upon myself and draw spiritual profit from it.

Second Point: I Will Listen to, Observe, and Contemplate What Mary and Joseph Are Saying

No complaints, no bitterness: "Let it be done to us according to God's will." I will listen to the exchange between them and the innkeeper: "There was no room for them in the place where travelers lodged." And then they finally found this cave-stable at the summit of a shepherd's field, much like the caves that one can see today in the Holy Land.

Then I will reflect upon myself and, I will draw spiritual profit from it.

Third Point: I Will Watch and Reflect on What They Are Doing

What a suffering-filled trip they are making! All of this so that the Lord will be born in poverty. And at the end of this journey, after all of the toil, the hunger and thirst, the heat and cold, the injustices and indignities, he is going to go and die on a Cross. And all of this for me.

Then I will reflect on myself and draw some spiritual profit from it.

I will talk over all of these things with Mary, Joseph, and the Infant Jesus, humbly, respectfully, even as a lowly servant would converse with his master.[1]

---

[1] This contemplation and the former exercise on the Incarnation can be made with great profit using the Application of the Senses. This is especially the case when either contemplation is made as a repetition.

THE HIDDEN LIFE AT NAZARETH

The Gospel *account* of this mystery (Luke 1:51–52) shows great reticence—because it is so profound a mystery. St. Ignatius presents it in this way:

1. Jesus was obedient to his parents. He grew in wisdom, age, and grace.

2. He appears to have practiced the trade of a carpenter, as St. Mark seems to imply: "Is this not the carpenter?" (Mark 6:3).

Place yourself in the presence of God and make the customary preparatory prayer.
Ask him to inspire you.

Composition of Place

The little town of Nazareth, and, in the midst of a neighborhood, the house of Joseph the carpenter.

I will ask for *what I want and desire.* Here it will be for an intimate knowledge of our Lord, who became man for me, so that I may love him more and follow him better.

The hidden life of Jesus at Nazareth is a "folly and scandal according to the flesh". We would like to emphasize here these three principal paradoxes.

First Paradox: A Self-Abasement More and More Profound on the Part of Christ Our Lord Parallel to His Growth in Human Values

1. A progressive self-effacement. We remember the gradual steps involved in this emptying out of the Word of God about which St. Paul spoke to the Philippians (2:6–11). Here are the first stages of this process, which he undertook himself: the Word was made flesh. He was born a tiny infant . . . in a humble, needy family. His boyhood was that of an apprentice . . . in a service trade. "And he was obedient to them", his father and mother.

2. Meanwhile, as he matured, he increased in a number of human virtues: "Size and strength, filled with wisdom, and the grace of God was upon him", as St. Luke recounts (2:39). He grew up and developed like all youngsters who are on the way to becoming adults. And he is God!

Second Paradox: For Christ Our Lord, the Recurrent Fluctuation of a Pattern of Death and Resurrection Was Already Present: In the Silence of Nazareth, the Redemption Comes About

1. Like the Philippians text to which we alluded, the various steps the Word of God took to empty himself out at Nazareth were balanced by the triumph of life and the glory of God.

"After all, you have died [to the ways of the world]! Your life is hidden now with Christ in God. When Christ our life appears, then you shall appear with him in glory" (Col 3:3–4). At Nazareth the hidden Christ lived in God and for God. And this is the way he saved the world.

2. At Nazareth, as in Jerusalem, as in his public life, as at Calvary, he is "about my Father's business". The important thing is not to do this or that. Rather, it is to be at the exact place God's Providence points out to us—through the different events that take place in our lives, our temperament, our age, our talents— where we should be. And we are to be there with the greatest amount of spiritual energy we can muster.

3. In the life of Christ our Lord there is a disproportion between the time of hidden silence (thirty years) and the time of public activity (three years). We see to which option God's heart is inclined. The silence of Nazareth is a silence filled with God, full with his will being accomplished with love—a silence of truth where all human falseness, artificiality, and appearances are done away with to the advantage of the Real—a silence filled with intimate conversations and simple encounters with the Father. The redemptive value of silence, obscurity, and of all the "nights".

Third Paradox: The Work and Prayer of the Trained Laborer

The craftsman, as symbol of the humble but effective coworker in God's creative labor . . . through his job, his toil, his insecurity, his service to his neighbor. His is a contribution to the world that is being made. What "worth" can be given to a carpenter at Nazareth? Much. Because here is where God placed him. He accomplished his task to the best of his ability, transforming it with his redemptive vision and with his prayer on earth.

What kind of Our Father must be that which Jesus, Mary, and Joseph say from the depths of their souls!

Nazareth is indeed the sum total of our life, the life of every person Christ has come to divinize. Tomorrow it may be the intense, exceptional mystery of the Passion. But today it is the sanctifying "little way": our ordinary work, our simple concerns, our meager efforts. The run-of-the-mill, ordinary people are a sacred people, a royal people. At Nazareth the Beatitudes are already prefigured.

In closing, *I will enter into conversation with:*

God the Father. I will adore him in his creation and in his Providence. I will tell him of my desire to "praise, reverence, and serve him" with my humdrum life, with the ordinary kind of work I do.

The Divine Child of Nazareth. I will tell him of my desire "to be with him" in humility, silence, work.

The Virgin Mary and St. Joseph . . . I will ask them for their faith in the mystery of Christ, the God made man.

I will say the Our Father in the company of Jesus, Mary, and Joseph. What a meaning Nazareth gives to the meditation on the first principle and foundation we made the first day of our retreat: man is created to love God, which is another way of saying that he "is created to praise, reverence, and serve God our Lord". Everything is love, That is, all can be summed up in terms of living for love, in love, and through love.

THIRTEENTH DAY

JESUS AMONG THE
DOCTORS OF THE TEMPLE

This contemplation and the previous one on the life of Jesus at Nazareth should also be seen as a diptych. The first contemplation depicted Jesus' obedience to his parents; here we will focus on his obedience to his Father in heaven.

Place yourself in the presence of God and make the customary prayer beginning the contemplation.
  I will call to mind the history of this mystery as it is recounted by St. Luke in 2:41–50.

Composition of Place

Here it will be the road that goes from Nazareth to Jerusalem and also the temple.
  I will ask for *what I want and desire:* here an interior knowledge of Christ our Lord, made man for me, so that I can love him more and serve him better.

First Point: Jesus Goes up to Jerusalem with His Parents to Celebrate the Passover There

I will see Mary and Joseph—and Jesus along with them—mingling with the nameless crowd of people on their way to the temple for the feast. I will imagine their spirit of prayer, their charity toward each other and the people they come in contact with, and their conversations.

Jesus, serious, reserved in the boyish manner of a twelve-year-old. And then:

— Before the temple . . . and all that that means for a young Jew, particularly for him: Would he not one day say, "Destroy this temple, and in three days I shall rebuild it"?

— Before the law: "I have come not to destroy the law but to fulfill it."

— Before Jerusalem . . . and during the Passover . . . what were his thoughts? Look at him closely. Between him and Mary there are periods of silence, exchanges of glances, charged with the future and fidelity to his Father in heaven.

Second Point: Jesus Remains in Jerusalem without His Parents' Knowing It

Joseph and Mary leave Jerusalem in the company of the caravan. The feast is over, and a large crowd forms again to leave the city. They have seen Jesus a number of times in the group, and so at the moment of departure they are not worried that he is not there with them.

Jesus makes a very serious decision. This is his hour for a first epiphany, for a first "transfiguration" during which something of his infinite wisdom will be revealed to the people about him. He remains at Jerusalem.

He stays behind. Let us think about this decision:

— He knew his parents would think that he was in the caravan bound for Nazareth.

— He knew that when they noticed his absence, they would be concerned, agonized, his Mother particularly.

— He knew that he was going to cause them pain, humiliation before their friends and acquaintances; cause them to bring their remorse in prayer to God.

Still, he stays on. It would have been simple for him to have told Mary and Joseph at the beginning of the pilgrimage to Jerusalem that the hour of God had arrived.

The mystery of Christ's silence, even in respect to his Mother.

He stayed on because one of "the works of his Father" was to be accomplished here, this day.

Third Point: After Three Days Joseph and Mary Found Jesus
Disputing in the Temple and Seated in the Midst of the Doctors

See this extraordinary scene: Jesus in the midst of the doctors of the law, listening to them, questioning them, astonishing them by his wisdom and by the intelligence of his answers. Listen . . . Savor the simplicity, the *truth,* the light of this young boy of twelve. And the doctors: if they knew that at this moment they are conversing with the Messiah, he who has come to fulfill the Scriptures that they spend time discussing but whose true secret is known by him alone . . .

For three days Mary and Joseph searched Jerusalem for Jesus: the anguish . . . the weariness . . . the remorse for what they considered their negligence. Then when they found him in the temple, what joy! "They were overcome when they saw him", the Gospel says.

Listen to the conversation between Mary and Jesus:

"Son, why have you done this to us? See how worried your father and I have been, looking for you."

"Why were you looking for me? Did you not know that I must be in my Father's house?"

Yes, they should have known that and thought about it immediately and reassured themselves in the certitude that Jesus would have left them only to be about "his Father's business". The gentle maternal reproach given Jesus by Mary is returned by a reproach on the part of Jesus to his Mother: she lacked confidence, faith, spiritual vision.

"But they did not understand what he meant." They did not yet grasp what he said, but they recorded his word in their heart, and there, at the very center of their being, that word will take life, germinate, and produce fruit: "His Mother stored up all these things in her heart."

I will talk over all of these things with Jesus our Lord, admiring him, questioning him, and listening to him, just as the doctors in the temple did. Then I will converse with Mary and Joseph.

I will end with an Our Father.

Preparation for Choosing to Order
My Life According to God's Love

We have meditated on the example that Christ our Lord has given us on the first state of life. This state consists in observing the Ten Commandments (he was obedient to his parents at Nazareth). Then we meditated on the example that the same Savior gave us of the second state of life, the state of *evangelical perfection* (leaving his Mother and foster father, he remained in the temple to devote himself exclusively to his eternal Father). While continuing to contemplate Christ's life, we are now going to focus on creating in ourselves the most favorable dispositions possible for making the choice to live our life according to the love of God alone.

This implies that we must make a completely free choice. It therefore means getting rid of any passion, any illusion, any pressure, so that we may come to a decision from our own reasoning, enlightened by faith and helped along by God's grace.

By way of introduction to our search to find God's will in our life so that we can make a choice—a search that will be prolonged over the following seven days of our thirty-day retreat—we are going to examine Christ our Lord's "intention", his plan for the world, in this next Exercise, and conversely, we shall also look at Satan's intention and his plan. In this Exercise we shall also see how we should order or dispose ourselves to genuine love in whatever state of life that God our Lord would will to place us here in this world.

But let us first state here precisely where we are in our retreat:

1. We have already made ourselves perfectly indifferent with

respect to all created things, and we have freely made the decision to prefer God to all things.

2. We have also chosen to respond, as far as we are able, with an unqualified Yes to the call of Christ our leader.

3. We know that the perfection of love can be found and reached in every state of life—married, single, religious. Christ our Savior was speaking to every Christian when he said, "Be perfect as your heavenly Father is perfect."

4. At this stage in the retreat, the retreatant is going to choose a state of life, or, if he has already made this choice, he will be asking himself what specific option he can make that will reform his life, thus making it better. Whether he fits in the first category or the second, the retreatant will be looking for what the will of God is in his life here and now. And he is going to do his best to respond to God's will realistically and with total honesty.

A MEDITATION ON TWO STANDARDS

*The One of Christ, Our Supreme Leader and Lord,
the Other of Lucifer, the Enemy of God and Man*

*Place yourself in the presence of God and make your preparatory prayer.
Ask him to inspire you.*

I Will Call to Mind the History

Using Ignatian imagery, I will consider the profound drama of
humanity. This consists, as St. John expresses it, in the struggle
between Darkness and Light, or in the thinking of St. Paul, in the
struggle between Spirit and Flesh, or as St. Augustine visualizes it,
in the struggle between the City of God and the City of Man. On
the one hand, I will picture Christ, who calls and who wishes to
unite all men, and on the other, I will imagine Lucifer, who draws
men away from Christ and makes them his own disciples.

Composition of Place

If it helps me, I will see in my imagination two plains. The first is
a great plain about Jerusalem, where our Lord, the sovereign
Leader of the "just", stands. The other plain is about the region of
Babylon, and here is where Lucifer, the enemy of Christ and the
enemy of our human nature, takes his place.

If this tableau seems to me to be too imaginative, I will picture
Christ our Lord before me. It is evening, and he appears tired after
a whole day of preaching. He is engaged in an evaluation of his

apostolate, balancing hostility or indifference (which he meets uninterruptedly and with every step he takes) with the love that he awakens in a number of hearts, the joy he communicates, and the glory that he gives to his Father.

I will ask for *what I want and desire.* Here I will ask for a knowledge of the tactics of Lucifer and for help and grace to guard myself against them. I will also ask for a knowledge of the *true life,* which our true and sovereign Leader, Jesus Christ, teaches, and for the grace to imitate him.

FIRST PART

First Point: I Will Imagine Lucifer in His Camp

If it helps, the retreatant should read the description of Lucifer in the twelfth chapter of the book of Revelation: "The huge dragon, the ancient serpent known as the devil or Satan, the seducer of the whole world". Or one can more simply, and with more realism, picture what the Gospel pejoratively calls "the world", using as an example some of our modern "Babylons": where Lucifer is with all his seductions, all his snares, all his tactics for lying and for blinding and even corrupting every man's conscience.

Second Point: I Will Consider Lucifer's Activity

He makes his presence universal, either directly or through his demons, or through perverse men—sending some to this city or that, throughout the whole world, so that no province, no place, no state of life, no single person is overlooked.

Consider the text: "Enraged at her [the Virgin Mary's] escape, the dragon went off to make war on the rest of her offspring, on those who keep God's commandments and give witness to Jesus."

Third Point: Lucifer's Tactics

Consider the discourse Lucifer addresses to those he scatters throughout the world. In essence it comes down to this: they are first of all to tempt men through their cravings for riches (this is the way it usually all begins) so that men will then more readily be carried away by the empty honors of this world and finally by overweening pride. Therefore, the first step is wealth and the power it brings; the second, worldly honor, and the third, pride. By these three passions, the devil will lead a man to all the other vices.

We recognize in this description the three "concupiscences" about which St. John writes (1 John 2:15–16): "If anyone loves the world, the Father's love has no place in him, because everything that there is in the world—disordered bodily desires, disordered desires of the eyes, pride in possession—is not from the Father, but it is from the world."

SECOND PART

We should now imagine Christ our Lord, our sovereign and true Chief, in a way that is the total opposite of Lucifer's.

First Point: I Will Consider Christ Our Lord

In the plain around Jerusalem where he so often traveled during his earthly life. His attitude is humble; his appearance handsome, attractive, nobleminded. Grace radiates from his whole person. He is one of those men who attract and fascinate others solely by the force of his presence; his enemies regarded him as a seducer.

Second Point: I Will Consider the Words That Christ Our Lord Addresses to All His Servants and Friends

As he sends them throughout the world, he commissions them to search out *all men of any and every condition and to help them* by:

1. First of all, attracting them to seek the highest spiritual poverty and, should the Divine Majesty be better served and would will it, even to embrace actual poverty.

2. And then leading them to the desire to strive for (or at least to esteem) humiliations and contempt. For it is from humiliations and contempt that a person is led to humility, that is, to a sense of reality about our human condition.

So there will be three steps in our approach to evangelical perfection:

— The first is poverty as opposed to riches.

— The second is humiliations and contempt as opposed to worldly honor.

— The third is humility as opposed to pride.

By these three steps, Christ's servants and friends lead men to all the other virtues.[1]

---

[1] We encounter again in this Meditation on Two Standards the problem that we have already seen in the meditation on the Kingdom, namely, are we dealing here with a normal or an exceptional type of Christianity? Our answer here is the same as it was previously: the call is one and is addressed to each Christian, but the response is different depending on the mystery of generosity in each soul. There are the "reasonable" people, who give themselves totally, all the while weighing their motives, which are, of course, good motives. Then there are those who wish to distinguish or signalize themselves, the *insignes,* and who give themselves freely, without any conditions attached. Finally, there are those still who hold themselves back and continue to throw themselves into the "vanity" of appearances. We will look at these various nuances later in all of the meditations touching on the election, that is, during practically the whole of the Second Week of the Exercises. It is up to each person to know himself, to weigh his own grace, and to respond with all his heart to the *"Dilexit me",* "he loved me . . . "

I will talk this matter over with our Lady, asking her that she obtain for me from her Son and Lord the grace to be received under his standard:

1. in the highest spiritual poverty and, should the Divine Majesty be better served and pleased to choose me, even in actual poverty;

2. so as to imitate him more, in accepting all the humiliations and injustices that come into my life, provided that I can take on these without causing anyone to sin and without offense to the Divine Majesty.

I will recite a Hail Mary.

I will make the same prayer to her Son, asking him to obtain for me the same graces from his Father. And I will say the prayer Soul of Christ.

I will ask the Father to grant me these same graces. And I shall say an Our Father.

FIFTEENTH DAY

THREE CLASSES OF MEN
*Faced with Making What Seems to Them
to Be the Best Decision*

This Exercise is made within the context of the Meditation on
Two Standards. Its purpose is to help us decide on the option that
seems to us to conform best to the will of God for us. St. Ignatius
chose poverty or the sincere desire to give up a certain amount of
money as a theme that has inspired this exercise. A person can also
substitute honors, success, a social position—anything that stands
for wealth and power in the eyes of men.

*Place yourself in the presence of God and make the prayer to begin the
exercise.*
  Ask him to inspire you.

I will place before my mind's eye the *history* St. Ignatius proposes.
There are three classes of men. Each one of them has acquired a
certain sum of money, but not solely from the love of God have
they become rich. All three groups wish "to save their souls" and
find the peace of God our Lord by freeing themselves from their
attachment to this money, which weighs heavy on them and
makes them feel uneasy. Hence they want to quiet their consciences.

Composition of Place

I will picture myself in the presence of God our Lord and all the
saints, eager that I may know and desire what is most pleasing to
his Divine Goodness for me.
  I will ask for *what I want and desire.* This will be the grace to

choose whatever is more for the glory of his Divine Majesty and whatever is better for the salvation of my soul.

First group. The men in this first group would like to rid themselves of the attachment they have to the sum of money so that they will be able to find the peace of God our Lord and save their souls. But they never find the means to do so before the hour of death overtakes them.

Second group. Those in the second group want to rid themselves of the attachment, but they wish to do so in such a way that they will keep the money. They want God to come around to what their position is. So they decide not to give up the money, not to go to God, even though a spontaneous surrender of the money would be the best course of action for them.

Third group. Those who are in the third group want to rid themselves of the attachment to the money, and they want to do it in such a way that they are not inclined either to keep it or to give it up. What they want is either to hold on to it or to give it up according to whatever God our Lord will inspire them to do and what will seem to them the better decision in terms of the greater service and praise of his Divine Majesty. Meanwhile, men in this class see themselves as being totally unattached to either one good or another. They try not to make a choice for either one or the other until they are impelled to do so by whatever they judge to be for the greater service of God alone. As a result of this decision, their desire is to be in a position where they can better serve God our Lord. It is on this basis that they keep or give up a particular good.[1]

---

[1] We should note that when we feel some attachment opposed to actual poverty or some repugnance toward it, when we are not indifferent to poverty or riches, it is very helpful to get rid of this inordinate attachment. We should beg in the colloquies, even in spite of our repugnances and feelings, that our Lord choose us to serve him in actual poverty, and we should insist that we want it and should plead for it, provided that it be to the service and praise of his Divine Goodness. It is indispensable to be rooted in total indifference if we want our choice of life to be an act of true spiritual liberty.

I shall talk over these matters at the end of this exercise with our Lady, with Christ our Lord, and with the Father, just as I did in the Meditation on the Two Standards.

SIXTEENTH DAY

THREE DEGREES OF HUMILITY:
THREE DEGREES IN THE LOVE OF GOD

The Meditation on the Two Standards has introduced us to the heart of the matter. We have seen how the world of its very nature is divided between good and evil, Christ and Satan, light and darkness, spirit and flesh. And so now comes the moment for the retreatant either to choose his state of life or to reform himself in the state of life he has already chosen.

In traditional spiritual language this choice is called "the election".

This election process will extend to all of the meditations and contemplations during the whole course of the Second Week.

As a final preparation for the election process, it will be most helpful for the retreatant to look at three methods of procedure that are designed to inculcate within him a sincere love of God. St. Ignatius and some other spiritual writers have designated these models the "degrees of humility". Actually, however, they are degrees of our love for God. We suggest that the retreatant reflect on them frequently during the day and that he pray peacefully the prayer recommended in the colloquies.

The First Degree or Kind of Humility: A Humility That Is Necessary for Salvation

It consists in this: that as far as possible I subject and humble myself to the degree that I obey the law of God our Lord in all things. The result will be that I would not consider breaking any one of the commandments of God or the Church that binds under the pain of *mortal sin,* even if I were to gain the whole world or even if my life depended on it.

This first sort of humility is of no small importance. It describes a person who already has a sincere attachment to the will of God, an authentic degree of love for God.

The Second Degree of Humility: Better Than the First

It consists in this: I have attained to this state of soul when I do not look for or seek riches as opposed to poverty, or honor rather than contempt, or a long life as opposed to a short one, provided that the service of God and the salvation of my soul be equally assured. With this kind of humility I would not consider committing one *venial sin,* not even for all creation, not even at the risk of saving my life. The person who has the second degree of humility is truly indifferent and can enjoy interior liberty, which is indispensable in making an election. He loves God with a very high degree of love in which, however, there is still a trace of legalism or excessive juridical thinking.

In these first two degrees of humility it is easy to identify the attitude of "the reasonable people" that was described in the contemplation of the Kingdom of Christ. Although love here is sincere and energetic, it does not yet realize what motivates it, and therefore it does not realize its capacity.

The Third Degree of Humility: the Most Perfect Humility

The third degree of humility corresponds to the love of the *insignes* in the contemplation of the Kingdom.

It includes the first and second type, but it adds to them this: in order better to imitate Christ our Lord and really be more like him, I want and choose poverty rather than riches; humiliations with Christ humiliated rather than honors, supposing that the praise and glory of the Divine Majesty be the same; and I prefer to be regarded as a man of no account and a fool *for Christ,* who was the first to pass for such, rather than be esteemed as a wise and prudent man in this world. The person who has this disposition goes beyond the stage of indifference; he has submitted to a personal love of Jesus Christ. This is the *"Nos stulti propter Christum"* (we are fools on Christ's account) of St. Paul (1 Cor 4:10). Let us call to mind here the "follies" of Francis of Assisi, Francis Xavier, the Curé d'Ars, etc., but let us also not forget the generosity of so many men and women who not only accept sorrows and pain and hardships in their lives but also rejoice in them because this "poverty" makes them resemble Jesus Christ all the more. Let us also call attention to the fact that if this inner disposition on the part of the retreatant is genuine and sane, it will not exclude his wanting to "cure" what is painful in his life, nor will it preclude any effort to escape from suffering. Rather, it means that if the effort proves unsuccessful, the person should rejoice that God permits him to participate so intimately in the sufferings of his Son. (See Note One: Penance, pp. 51–53.)

Colloquies. An excellent exercise for the person who wishes to attain to this third kind of humility will be to remake the three colloquies from the Meditation on the Two Standards. In these he should beg our Lord to be pleased to choose him for this third degree so that he may imitate him better and serve him more, provided that equal or greater service and praise be given to his Divine Majesty.

On Making a Choice of a Way
of Life According to God's Will

PREAMBLE

In every good election, as far as it depends on us, our intention ought to be simple. I should consider only the end for which I was created: the praise of God our Lord and the salvation of my soul. Therefore, whatever choice I make should be such as to help me reach this end. I ought not to subordinate the end to the means but the means to the end.

For example, many decide first of all to marry (which is an end) and then choose the service of God in marriage. There are others who want first to embrace this particular career and afterward to serve God in it. Such persons do not go straightaway to God, but they want God to come directly to their inordinate attachments. They make a means of the end and an end of the means. What they ought to put in first place they in fact put in second place. Good order requires that we first of all want to serve God, who is our end, and after that we then decide to embrace this career, or to get married, and so forth, *because* this choice *for us* is really the best means to love God and to serve him in others.

What Are the Matters about Which
a Person Should Make an Election?

1. The matters about which we should make an election evidently ought to be good or at least indifferent in themselves and approved by our holy mother, the hierarchical Church, that is to say, they should not be bad or contrary to the Church.

2. There are some choices that fall under the category of being made once and for all: choices such as the priesthood, being married, and the like. Others are choices that can be changed, for example, accepting some obligation, acquiring or relinquishing property.

3. In the case of an unchangeable choice, once it has been made, no further choice can be considered because it cannot be undone (for instance, marriage, the priesthood, and the like). The only thing to be said here is that if this election was not made as it should have been, that is to say, if it was made in conjunction with inordinate attachments, one should be sorry for having made it, and then he should continue living a good life along the path that was poorly chosen. But we should not consider this election as a vocation that conforms to the will of God since it was a faulty election. There is a great deal of erroneous thinking in this matter. A vocation that comes from God is pure and undefiled, without any admixture of sensuality or inordinate attachments.

4. On the one hand, when one deals with an election that can be changed by the person who has made the choice correctly, that is to say, he made it without compromising with the views and principles of the world, there is no place for making a further choice. In this case he should make the effort to conduct himself

the best way he can within the framework of the choice he has made.

5. But on the other hand, if this choice was made about matters that are subject to change and was made in a dishonest and disordered way, there is an advantage to remaking the choice in a correct way so that it will bring forth an abundant harvest and will thereby be pleasing to God our Lord.

Three States of the Soul When a
Sound and Solid Choice of a Way of Life May Be Made

The first state occurs when God our Lord moves and attracts the will of a faithful soul in such a manner that precludes all doubt concerning who is calling him and what he is being called to do. He then follows the way that has been shown to him. This was how St. Paul (Acts 9) and St. Matthew (Matt 9:9) responded.

The second state occurs when the soul has been given sufficient light and understanding through consolations and desolations and through the discernment of spirits. (See pp. 221–29.)

The third state occurs when the soul is at peace. The person making the choice considers first of all why he was born, which is to praise God our Lord and to save his soul. In his desire to attain this end, he chooses one of the states of life approved by the Church as the means to the end.

I call being at peace that state when the soul is not agitated by different spirits but, with the concurrence of the Holy Spirit, uses its natural powers freely and unperturbedly.

If the person making the election is not among those described in the first or second state of the soul, there are two ways to make a choice. These remarks pertain to those who fit into the category of the third state of the soul.

FIRST WAY OF MAKING A GOOD AND SOUND CHOICE
WHEN THE SOUL IS AT PEACE

1. I put the matter of the choice before me—for example, a particular charge I am considering taking on or leaving or any

other matter that falls under the category "changes I am free to make".

2. It is helpful to keep before my eyes the purpose for which I was created: to praise our Lord and save my soul. Furthermore, I must remain *indifferent,* without any inordinate attachments, so that I do not have any more inclination or desire to choose one option and reject another than I do to reject one and choose the other. I shall remain like a swinging needle of a compass, poised to turn toward what I feel will conform most to the glory and praise of God our Lord and the salvation of my soul.

3. I shall then beg God our Lord to be pleased to move my will and let me know interiorly what I ought to do to praise and glorify him more when faced with the choice I am considering and that in the light of this knowledge he will enable me first to make an exact and faithful examination of the matter before me, and then that he will enable me to proceed in making my choice according to his holy will and good pleasure.

4. Afterward I shall mull over in my mind and will weigh the advantages and benefits that would come solely for the praise of God our Lord and for the good of my soul in each case, for example, if I were to keep a particular responsibility or not. Then I would do the opposite, weighing the disadvantages and dangers that would accrue by my holding on to this charge.

Then I shall repeat the process, this time by considering the advantages and benefits that would come from giving up the responsibility and then considering the disadvantages and dangers that would result.

5. After analyzing and debating the problem with all the pros and cons in this way, I shall consider which of the alternatives seems the most reasonable. This way I shall come to make my choice because of healthy, reasonable motives as opposed to some kind of emotional intuition.

6. After making my choice, I shall most eagerly place it before

God our Lord in prayer, and, offering him my choice, I shall pray that if it is for his greater service and glory, his Divine Majesty may be pleased to accept and confirm my choice.

THE SECOND WAY OF MAKING A GOOD AND SOUND CHOICE WHEN THE SOUL IS AT PEACE

First rule. The love that moves me and causes me to make my choice must descend from on high, from the love of God; therefore the person who makes a choice must feel within himself that the only motive for his preference in making his choice is this love for his Creator and Lord.

Second rule. I shall imagine a man whom I have never seen or known but who is in a situation similar to my own and for whom I would wish every possible blessing. And I shall think about what I would advise him in making his choice for the greater glory of God our Lord and for the greater progress of his soul.

Third rule. I shall imagine that I am at the point of death, and I shall consider what inclinations and attitudes I would have liked to have had then when I was making the present election. I shall go entirely by the results of this consideration in deciding how I should now make my choice.

Fourth rule. I shall imagine myself at Judgment Day. I shall then ask myself what decision would I have wished to have made concerning the matter at hand. The rule of conduct I would have wished to have followed then I shall adopt now, so that when I am judged I shall be able to enjoy complete happiness and sheer joy over my decision.

Fifth rule. Now that I have put into effect the rules given above, which are meant for my salvation and eternal repose, I shall make my election. And when I have made it, I shall waste no time in bringing it in prayer to the presence of God our Lord, offering it to him so that his Divine Majesty may be pleased to receive and confirm it, if such a reception and confirmation are to his greater service and praise.

TWO VERY IMPORTANT NOTES

1. It seems to me that it is against all reason to set up a hierarchy among the three types of election. God guides souls as he wishes. Is St. Peter of lesser importance than St. Paul because he was not thrown to the ground on the road to Damascus? And just because St. Francis de Sales heard God's call from his boyhood days, does this mean he is less entitled to be a spiritual guide than the converted sinner St. Ignatius? Just asking such questions is to answer them!

2. In number 6 of the First Way of Making a Choice (pp. 130–31) and in the fifth rule of the Second Way of Making a Choice (p. 131), Ignatius uses the words *to confirm* and *confirmation* of a person's choice by the Holy Spirit. This idea could cause difficulties for the director and the retreatant. What does *interior confirmation* by the Holy Spirit mean? We follow the wise interpretation given by Father Joseph de Guibert, S.J.,[1] who writes that after the choice is made, a positive confirmation should not be excluded; however, the term refers to a negative confirmation, by which he means that if God does not indicate to me interiorly that my choice is contrary to his will, I shall consider it as being conformed to his will. This way of interpreting the inspirations of the Holy Spirit seems to me to conform best to a reasonable theological understanding of the relationship between human reason and the light of faith.

SUGGESTIONS FOR THE REFORM
OF ONE'S LIFE AND SPIRITUAL PROGRESS

It is possible that some of the people who will make this retreat are already committed to a permanent state of life, such as marriage, or the priesthood, and there may be others who do not have the

---

[1] *The Theology of the Spiritual Life,* trans. Paul Barrett, O.F.M. Cap. (New York: Sheed & Ward, 1953), 118–19.

opportunity or desire to make a choice on matters that may be changed. The methods for making a choice that we have outlined here will still be very useful in helping such retreatants better reform their lives.

As a way to set out in this direction and attain this end, every retreatant might use the exercises and methods of election indicated above to help him give a religious dimension to his life— how he should conduct his affairs and how he ought to give witness by word and example to his Christian commitment among those persons with whom he comes in contact each day. He might also use them to examine himself on how much of his time, energy, and money he should reserve for his family, his work, and his community and how much he should give to the poor and to different Church-related activities. As the criterion for what he does, let him desire and look for nothing beyond the greater praise and glory of God our Lord. He should remind himself that he will make progress in his Christian life in proportion as he surrenders selfishness and seeks simply the Kingdom of God in all his undertakings.

Let us also note that these guidelines for making a choice can be used outside of the retreat as well—in those situations that call for decisions in the everyday social, familial, and even professional life of the Christian.

SEVENTEENTH DAY

JESUS IN THE DESERT

Even though I have made my election, I shall continue making meditations designed to impress upon me the spirit of Jesus Christ.

Put yourself in the presence of God and make the preparatory prayer. Ask him to inspire you.

I will call to mind the *history* of this mystery (see Luke 4:1–13 or Matt 4:1–11).

Composition of Place

The desert: Jesus alone. After his baptism by John the Baptist, Jesus is led by the Holy Spirit to the desert, where he fasts forty days and forty nights. He is tempted three times by Satan. After he overcomes this triple temptation, angels come and wait on him.

I will ask for *what I want and desire:* an intimate knowledge of Christ our Lord, who is made man for me, so that I may love him more and follow him more closely.

First Point: After He Had Been Baptized by John the Baptist, Jesus Went to the Desert, Where He Fasted Forty Days and Forty Nights

1. I will consider Jesus wanting solitude before beginning his encounter with men . . . eager to come face to face again with his Father . . . his joy . . . his eternity. At the hour of his Passion, he will say, "I can never be alone; the Father is with me" (John 16:32). Yet here, now, in this mystery, he says it already.

2. This being alone with the Father is really the true "place" for Jesus. The forty days in the desert are the prelude to all those times he prayed during the night that the Gospels will tell us about.

3. Listen to this prayer of Christ and savor it. It is a filial prayer, a prayer in which he places himself at the service of the Father, offering himself unreservedly for the Father's mission, with perfect freedom of his will and total unselfishness. His only will is to do the Father's holy will. This is pure love, the love of the Son for his Father.

4. It is the Holy Spirit who "leads Jesus to the desert". He is the one who is the great designer of God's activity in the souls of men and in the world.

5. Jesus fasts for forty days. I will scrutinize him here. I will ask myself why he fasts. I will think about the demands of penance on every person who strives to experience true prayer and the "interior freedom" of the children of God. Fasting is the symbol of a total rejection of our attachment to the good things of this earth; it turns the soul toward "heavenly food". To hunger for justice . . . to hunger for God. After his meeting with the Samaritan woman (John 4:32), Jesus said to his disciples, "I have food to eat of which you do not know." Yet here the Gospel tells us, "At the end of his fast he was hungry." Jesus is as truly man as we are.

Second Point: He Was Tempted by Satan Three Times

We will contemplate this "temptation" of Jesus. It is directed toward our instruction and profit.

Let us listen to the dialogue, going deep into the heart of the two actors in this scene in order to understand interiorly the integrity and loyalty of Jesus our Chief, on the one hand, and on the other, the wiliness and ruses of Satan. We have here acted out before us the Meditation on the Two Standards in which we have the following elements:

1. There is the temptation to live a dazzling, magical, exceptional life: "If you are the Son of God, command this stone to turn into bread." "Scripture has it, 'Not on bread alone shall man live.'" Jesus, the son of the carpenter, will live as ordinary people live, taking his place in society as a man like each of us.

2. There is the temptation to amass worldly power: "I will give you all this power and the glory of these kingdoms." "You shall do homage to the Lord your God; him and him alone shall you adore." Jesus seeks only the Kingdom of God, the glory of his Father.

3. There is the temptation to dazzle and seduce the crowds: "If you are the Son of God, throw yourself down from here, for Scripture has it, 'He will bid his angels watch over you.' ... Jesus said to him in reply, 'It also says, "You should not put the Lord your God to the test."'" Jesus would perform miracles only "to give glory to his Father", at the hour fixed by his Father, in the circumstances that God's Providence would dictate. He would not "tempt" his Father but would obey him.

4. Finally, we should take note of the fact that Jesus fends off Satan's temptations by citing Scripture (the eternal Word of God), but also that when Satan tries to seduce Jesus, he too makes use of the words of Scripture. Reflect on the description of the dialogue between Jesus and Satan.

Third Point: "When the Devil Had Finished All the Tempting He Left Him, to Await Another Opportunity", Says St. Luke. St. Mark and St. Matthew Add, "And Angels Waited on Him"

Jesus has unmasked the ruses of Lucifer. But the struggle between Jesus and Lucifer will go on for three more years. Lucifer will have his hour of victory—during the Passion. But all will end with his final defeat and the definitive victory of Christ. The Meditation on Two Standards is not a fable but the real, everyday, historical reality, the very warp and woof out of which our lives are made.

Contemplate the peace that prevails in the final scene: Jesus surrounded by the "celestial choir". He is served by angels.

In closing, *I will talk these matters over* with Jesus our Lord. I will ask him for the grace that I too may encounter solitude, silence, prayer, and moderate but nevertheless authentic penance, for it is in such a "desert" that my soul will most truly and surely find him.

I will say the Our Father.

THE VOCATION AND FORMATION OF THE APOSTLES

The retreatant making this contemplation has the choice of taking one of the New Testament scenes — or indeed all of the scenes — depicting Jesus calling one or another of his apostles: his first meeting with Peter and Andrew (John 1:35–42); their total definitive commitment to him (Matt 4:18–22; Mark 1:16–20); the call of Philip (John 1:43–44) and Matthew (Matt 9:9).

The vocation of the apostles obviously captured the attention of St. Ignatius, who added the following note, which we should keep in mind:

"We can consider this call under three aspects: (1) that the apostles were unschooled and from a humble background, (2) the dignity to which they were so gently called, and (3) that the gifts and graces they were given raised them above all of the Fathers of the Old and New Testaments." In these few lines we have the whole connotation of what we mean by "the apostles".

We are going to present in this contemplation the scene from Luke 6:12–16 where Jesus "called his disciples and selected twelve of them to be his apostles", and we will follow up on this call with Mark 3:13–19 and Matthew 10:1–4.

Place yourself in the presence of God and make the beginning prayer.
Ask him to inspire you.

I will call to mind the *history* of this event as it is described in the Gospel. Jesus tore himself away from everyone and went off by himself to the mountain; here he spent the night in prayer. At daybreak he called his disciples and chose twelve from among them to be with him so that he could send them to preach the good news; he gave them the power to expel demons.

Composition of Place

We are along the banks of Lake of Gennesaret: the flat lands follow the shoreline, and the mountain is in the background.

I will ask for *what I want and desire:* an intimate knowledge of Christ our Lord, who was made man for me, so that I can love him, follow him, and serve him more. Or in the words of St. Ignatius at La Storta, I will ask for the grace "to be with Jesus Christ" ("to be with him", as the Gospel says).

First Point: The Call of the Twelve

I will take a part in this scene.

1. What are the constituent parts of this call? He chose them after spending the whole night in prayer. He constituted them

— To be with him.

— To be sent out by him to preach. Later on St. Paul would say of him, "He sent me to preach the Gospel" (1 Cor 1:17).

— And to heal and to expel demons.

2. We already know a number of the Twelve who were chosen:

— John and Andrew (John 1:40–42),

— Simon, who was named Peter, that is, "Rock" (John 1:40–42),

— Philip and Nathanael (John 1:43–51),

— Simon, Andrew, John, and James (Luke 5; Mark 1; Matt 4) (the miraculous catch of fish, the fishermen's nets, fishers of men ...)

— Matthew (Levi) (Matt 9; Mark 2; Luke 4).

We still do not know the others at this point. We should take note of the terrible phrase of the Synoptics: "And Judas Iscariot who turned traitor". The mystery of God's choices!

Second Point: What Jesus Made of His Apostles

1. Even though he gave them no other "vocation" than that of being his disciples—all are called to be "sons of God".

2. Nevertheless he gave them

— an intimacy with him in his work of redemption; he made them his "coworkers", collaborators; he invited them to live the "with me" with a greater intensity;

— all his powers to teach, sanctify, govern, to be other Christs in this world. The hierarchy of the Church is inaugurated here; the ministerial priesthood is already outlined.

In short, what we have here already is the teaching "not to be worried and not to fret about so many things, for few things are necessary, indeed, only one", the *unum necessarium,* the coming of the Kingdom of God here below.

Such is the vocation of the apostle—a vocation that can unfortunately one day be disclaimed: Judas.

Third Point: What Is the Type of Education That Jesus Gave His Apostles to Enable Them to Pass from Their "Unschooled and Humble Backgrounds" to the Quality of Being Apostles?

Like all the Jews of their time, these men espoused the dream of restoring the Kingdom of Israel: a temporal kingdom that would be powerful and rich. They had to progress to the idea of the Kingdom of the eternal King in the Meditation on Two Standards, that is, a Kingdom that is spiritual, humble, poor, charitable, willing to mete out forgiveness.

This progression, this gradual purification of their dream, which allowed them to enter through *faith* into the true Kingdom of God, sums up the whole drama in the formation of the apostles.

The progress took place slowly.

Unquestionably Jesus got some clear and consoling results, such as Peter's confession at Caesarea Philippi; the fidelity of the Twelve after the discourse on the Bread of Life at Capernaum; the transfiguration; Peter's protestation when Jesus wanted to wash his feet.

But even after the Passion and Resurrection, the old dream of a temporal kingdom remained with them: one time before the ascension "when appearing to them over the course of forty days ... they asked, 'Lord, are you going to restore the rule to Israel now?' " (Acts 1:6).

Only the Holy Spirit would at last transform them ... Pentecost ... a very short time after the descent of the Holy Spirit, Peter and the apostles began to preach. They preached about the death and Resurrection of Christ, and about the true Kingdom of God. They faced up to the wise and powerful of this world, but they were armed with only the peaceful and formidable weapons of God's strength and goodness.

In ending my prayer, *I will converse*

— with Jesus Christ, asking him to "choose" me for true and sincere love; never to let me betray him but to love and serve him.

— with Peter, an apostle to whom I feel so much akin.

I will recite the Our Father.

THE BEATITUDES

There is no question about it: the best way for us to penetrate into the spirit of Christ our Lord is to meditate slowly on the Sermon on the Mount. Today, then, we will pause to consider the Beatitudes, which Matthew places at the beginning of this Sermon (5:3–16). These Beatitudes sound the theme running through the whole sermon (and we should not divorce them from the "woe to you" verses found in St. Luke 6:24–26).

Put yourself in the presence of God and make the prayer for beginning the meditation.
    Ask him to inspire you.

I will call to mind the *history of the mystery:* after the long years of preparation he spent in the hidden life, after his baptism in the Jordan, the time of penance in the desert, his first preaching experiences, Jesus today is going to promulgate his law and will present the first organizational draft of his plan of action. He has passed the night in prayer. In the early morning he chose the Twelve. He comes down now to the shoreline. The crowds begin to assemble. He retraces his steps a bit up to the higher ground.

Composition of Place

The crowds of people take their places along the shoreline of the Lake of Gennesaret. Some are seated in the typical fashion of the Near East; others are standing. Jesus has selected a little incline up from and facing his audience, and from here he will begin speaking like a doctor of the law. It is springtime in Galilee. Jesus raises his eyes and sees the crowds that press in upon him and have now become silent. Behind the people is the clear, blue lake. Beyond it, and along the horizon on the opposite shore, rise up the mountains where the city of Safed is built. Seated there Jesus dominates all reality, all ages, all the worlds.

I will ask for *what I want and desire:* either for the grace of the Kingdom: "Not to be deaf to his call but prompt and diligent to do his most holy will"; or for the grace of the Two Standards: "An understanding of the true life, which the true and supreme Chief teaches, and the grace to follow him more closely".

First Point: Beati: *Blessed Be . . .*

Appreciate the melodious, irresistible force that this word has on the hearts of these men and women who make up the crowds listening to Jesus; on the human heart today.

1. Be careful, however, not to give this word *blessed* a soft, sweetish connotation. André Gide said that Christianity was *"une religion de pleutres"* (a religion for wimps). No, it is not that. The sufferings and the hardships of those who are listening to Christ here would never stand for that. It is just the opposite with them: they have a firm desire for happiness. Feel that same sentiment alive in the people of today's world.

2. Jesus immediately situates this blessedness only where it can be really found, that is, in the Kingdom of heaven.

"The Kingdom of God is theirs" is the opening and closing sentence of the Beatitudes. In between we have: "They shall see God" . . . "They shall be recognized as the children of God" . . . "consoled . . . satisfied", "They shall have mercy shown to them", "They shall have *the earth* as their inheritance."

This is a new earth, a new order, new values that Jesus is going to set up: supernatural, of course, but also a world of creation restored in peace and charity—or at least it is one that will tend toward this restoration because of the thrust he gives it . . . leaven . . . salt . . . light of the world. What if these Beatitudes were the charter for our world here on earth? What a change there would be in our dealings with one another!

3. We should not forget that there are two possible responses to this invitation on the part of the Lord to live the Beatitudes: the response of those we called "reasonable" above—people who understand that the Beatitudes can be the wisdom of man and at the same time the wisdom of God (and this is very beautiful and very true!). And then there is the response of the *insignes*. These accept the position of the reasonable, but they want to go beyond their arguments and choose the Person of Christ our Lord, his way, his Cross. *"Dilexit me"* (he loved me).

4. I will try to appreciate all of this by considering the joy that Christ our Lord promises and brings to the world: his joy, his complete, abundant joy. . . . *May my joy live on!*
Joy should be "the gigantic secret of those who believe in Jesus"—the joy of those who have conquered.

5. This is really the way that the crowds understand the words of Jesus. (Cf. Matthew's account of the effect of the Sermon on the Mount [7:28-29]: "Jesus had now finished what he wanted to say, and his teaching made a deep impression on the people because he taught them with authority, unlike their own scribes.")

Second Point: Who Are These "Blessed" of the Sermon on the Mount?

They are the mistreated of this life, victims of political systems, rejects of pharisaical religions: fishermen, publicans, laborers who subsist on what they make from one day to the next. They are the *minores*, the *ptôkoi:* they are all lumped together under the category of "the poor".

The first Beatitude summarizes the rest because those that follow are simply repeating the first under different names. The first Beatitude can be called the Beatitude of those with empty hands. The central law of the spiritual life is this: we must always come before God with empty hands. Grace is a gratuitous gift.

Christ takes up the word *poor* in the sense it was already given by the prophet Zephaniah (2:3): "Seek the Lord, all you humble of the earth. . . . Seek justice and humility." In another place, St. Matthew would call them "the poor in spirit". The "humble", the ill-provided and oppressed, are more open to the Kingdom of heaven than the powerful and rich. But "poverty", in order to be the poverty of the Beatitudes, has to be seized onto for one's own use, freely accepted in a direction of truth and interior liberty.

Here in this consideration we are thrust once more into the dynamics of the Meditation on the Two Standards.

Third Point: The Beatitude of Christ

The model, source, and ideal of these "blessed" is Christ our Lord himself.

All his life he practiced the Beatitudes.

They represent his spirit, his teaching, his law.

He came to communicate to men the beatitudes he enjoyed as Son: "Father, the hour has come! Give glory to your Son"; and why? "So that your Son may give glory to you, inasmuch as . . . he may bestow eternal life on those you gave him . . . that they may share my joy completely."

But let us not forget that in regaining for us his joy through his Resurrection, Christ our Lord first had to pass through his "self-abasements", that is, the Incarnation, the obedience he showed to human authority, and his death on the Cross. And me, what will I do for Jesus Christ, who has loved me so much?

I will end my meditation by *talking over all of these matters* with Jesus Christ. I will savor his bliss, his beatitude. I will restate my faith in his Word: "Lord," I will repeat myself what St. Peter said to you, "to whom should we go? You have the words of eternal life." Appreciate what this certainty really implies by spending a long time considering its implications.

I will recite the Our Father, which is part of the Sermon on the Mount.[1]

[1] A reconsideration of the material in this meditation on the true spirit of poverty for the Christian living in the world—indeed, the most balanced and most realistic account—can be found in chaps. 14 through 16 of "The Practice of Virtue", St. Francis de Sales, *Introduction to the Devout Life,* 128–35.

THE TRANSFIGURATION

According to many authorities of the spiritual life this mystery is the most significant event that took place during the public life of Christ because it is here that Christ lifts the veil of his self-effacement and thereby manifests himself to us, showing us at the same time who he really is, namely, the Word Made Flesh, and what his role, mission, and glory are.

Place yourself in God's presence and make your beginning prayer.
   Ask him to inspire you.

I will call to mind the *history* of this mystery: we are at the zenith of the public life of Christ our Lord. Peter has just "confessed" his faith in Christ at Caesarea Philippi. Jesus announced his Resurrection for the first time and then stated explicitly, "If a man wishes to come after me, he must deny his very self, take up his cross, and begin to follow in my footsteps" (Matt 16:24). "Six days later" (17:1) the transfiguration took place.

Composition of Place

Jesus climbed up a mountain (Mount Tabor, according to Tradition) with Peter (the Primate), John (the disciple whom he loved), and James (the first of the apostles who would give testimony to Jesus by shedding his blood; Acts 12:2).

I will ask for *what I want and desire:* an intimate knowledge of Christ our Lord, who, "veiling over his prerogatives as God", was made man for me. And I will ask for a greater love and a more

147

effective desire to imitate him by taking up my cross each day.

First Point: The Transfiguration

1. Jesus ascends the mountain to pray. He brings Peter, James, and John with him.

Prayer: the contact of *faith* with the invisible world . . . being immersed in the Real, the divine. Jesus' prayer at Tabor is a prelude to another prayer—that of Gethsemane, where he will be with the same three apostles. But on that night they will not be able to keep company with him in his agony; their eyes will be too heavy with exhaustion and emotion, and so they will sleep. Let us try to appreciate the atmosphere of death and mortification that introduces this scene of glory and joy. Six days previously Jesus had solemnly announced his death, and he asked the person wanting to follow him to be willing to take up his cross (Luke 9:23).

2. The event:

Luke: "His face changed in appearance, and his clothes became dazzling white" (9:29).

Mark: "He was transfigured before their eyes, and his clothes became dazzling white—whiter than the work of any bleacher could make them" (9:2–3).

Matthew: "He was transfigured before their eyes. His face became dazzling as the sun, his clothes as radiant as light" (17:2).

See, relish, admire this splendor of Christ. It filled his soul.

The transformation that took place in Christ is not a change like that which occurs in the grain of wheat that mutates so as to give life to the sprout, nor is it in any way similar to the chrysalis that is metamorphosed into a butterfly. Rather it is a sudden revelation of what is already there, like a light that suddenly shines forth from some hidden place where it had been covered over.

The real problem is not how the transfiguration took place but rather how it was that this glory did not show itself the moment the Word was made flesh. How was it that the glory of the Word did not shine forth from his body all the time? Jesus wanted to save us by taking on our sinful flesh, "the wretched body of ours" (Phil 3:21). He became man not as playacting or as appearance only but out of true love.

3. The presence of Moses (the law) and Elijah (the prophets): These two figures had risked their lives for God: Moses before the Pharaoh (Exod 3:10; 5:1) and Elijah before Ahab (1 Kings 17:1). Their presence is a tribute of respect to our Savior's Passion.

"They . . . spoke of his passage, which he was about to fulfill in Jerusalem" (Luke 9:31).

Through his Cross Jesus came to "fulfill" the law and the prophets; he did not come abolish them (Matt 5:17). This fact explains the presence of Moses and Elijah at his transfiguration. Jesus is greater than Moses and Elijah, who simply announced his coming.

4. The "human" reaction of Peter: "Master, how good it is for us to be here. Let us set up three booths, one for you, one for Moses, and one for Elijah" (Luke 9:33). Mark excuses Peter's reaction by adding, "He hardly knew what to say" (Mark 9:6). Hear Peter speaking; contemplate him in his awe and confusion.

Jesus could have answered him with what he had already told him on another occasion: "Get out of my sight, you satan! You are trying to make me trip and fall" (Matt 16:23), because his suggestion was going against the plan of redemption.

In spite of the recent "confession" he had made at Caesarea Philippi, a confession that was so clear and formal ("You are the Christ, the Son of the living God"), Peter still had a long way to go before he arrived at true faith. Jesus is gentle in the education of souls, patient in the education of *our* souls!

5. The voice from heaven, the theophany:

This voice from heaven calls to mind the theophany at our

Lord's baptism in the Jordan. There, as here, the Father introduces his Son. The parallel is suggestive. (We should observe that there was nothing "dazzling" about Christ at his baptism.)

While Jesus was speaking to Moses and Elijah, "a cloud came and overshadowed them" (Luke 19:34). The cloud in Scriptural symbolism tells of the mysterious and efficacious presence of the invisible God. It was the cloud that miraculously led the Hebrews out of Egypt and far from Pharaoh (Exod 12:21), and it was the cloud that "covered the Tent of the Meeting, and the glory of Yahweh filled the tabernacle" (Exod 40:34).

6. The three apostles were overcome with fear. They fell forward on the ground (Matt 17:6).

Let us recall what Moses did when God revealed his presence in the burning bush: "Moses hid his face, for he was afraid to look at God" (Exod 3:6). One day we shall see God face to face. What distance!

Jesus raised up the apostles. He came toward them. He touched them and said, "Rise up! Do not be afraid" (Matt 17:7). "Do not be afraid": already a Resurrection word!

Second Point: The Meaning of the Transfiguration

This mystery is at the heart of our vocation as sons of God. What we are is infinitely more beautiful than what we seem to be. Our life unfolds on two levels: that of appearances, of signs, of "things visible"; and on the "invisible" level of divine reality within us, of our "glory"—the shadowy part and the luminous part of the one and the selfsame reality. At times the Lord permits something of the invisible reality of his presence and glory clearly to be experienced from within, or he allows us to see it in some activity in which we are engaged. But it is in the ordinary where our life of faith and hope is lived.

We can read with profit such texts as:

— 1 John 3:2 (the "manifestation" of what we are),

— Colossians 3:2–4 (our "manifestation" with Christ),

— 2 Corinthians 4:17 (the present burden is light in comparison with eternal glory),

— Philippians 3:20–21 (the "transfiguration" of our lowly body into a glorified body),

— 1 Corinthians 25:51 (we will be "transformed").

Heaven, our heaven, is already in us, now, this very day: "God has made his dwelling place in us" (John 14:23).
"Yes . . . ! Come, Lord Jesus, come!" (Rev 22:20).

Third Point: Only Jesus

Luke: "And after the voice had spoken, Jesus was found alone" (11:36).

Mark: "Suddenly looking around they no longer saw anyone with them—only Jesus" (9:8).

Matthew: "When they looked up they did not see anyone but Jesus" (17:8).

"Jesus"—only, but it is enough. What difference is it if it is Jesus of the *"kenosis"*, of his self-effacements, or Jesus in his glory?

To be "with him" is enough for me.

"Jesus"—an excellent invocation; it is the prayer that says all. Compare the "prayer of the heart" in the first centuries of the Church and among the Christians of the East.

"Jesus"—as the Church prays: *"Per Dominum Nostrum Jesum Christum"* (through our Lord Jesus Christ), or, as St. Paul prays in his unparalleled expression: *"In Christo Jesu"*.

I will converse with Christ our Lord about these things in a fervent colloquy. I will take part, with humility, in the extraordinary conversation between Jesus, Moses, and Elijah. I will attempt to understand a bit better the relationship between glory and the Cross in the mystery of Jesus.

TWENTY-FIRST DAY

THE RAISING OF LAZARUS

Among Christ our Lord's miracles, perhaps none is more striking than the raising of Lazarus. Most assuredly no other page of the Gospel better reveals the human tenderness of our Lord's heart.

Place yourself in God's presence and make your beginning prayer.
Ask him to inspire you.

I will call to mind the *history of the miracle* with the help of St. John (11:1–45). Martha and Mary of Bethany have just advised Jesus that Lazarus, their brother and his friend, is very sick. Jesus tarries two days before responding to their call. In the meanwhile Lazarus dies. By the time Jesus arrives at Bethany, Lazarus has already been in the tomb four days. Jesus raises him from the dead.

Composition of Place

First of all, there is Jesus somewhere in Galilee. Then there is the house of his friends at Bethany, a stopping-off place for him when he is in the neighborhood. Finally, there is the tomb of Lazarus.

I will ask for *what I want and desire:* here it will be to know better the human heart of Christ our Lord so that I can love him better in return and imitate him more closely.

First Point: Lazarus Is Sick

1. The first course of action Martha and Mary take is to inform Christ our Lord about Lazarus: "Lord, the one you love is sick."

Will not he who has cured so many sick people intervene to save the one he loves? Merely to notify Jesus is enough to obtain a miracle—or so Lazarus' two sisters think.

2. But Jesus does not set off for Bethany. He stays in the place where he received the message for at least two more days. There are two opposing sentiments in his heart:

"Jesus loved Martha and her sister and Lazarus very much" (John 11:5). He knows that his absence will surprise them, even hurt them. He knows that Lazarus is going to die and that Martha and Mary will be sorely crushed.

However, "This sickness . . . is for God's glory, that through it the Son of God may be glorified" (John 11:4). From that moment on, there is no hesitation for him because God's glory comes before the most sacred of human sentiments. Jesus accepts the fact that for a while he may be taken for heartless, a fair-weather friend, one who is for all practical purposes unreliable.

Second Point: Jesus Returns to Bethany

1. "Let us go back to Judea." His decision is courageous because the Jews are looking for him. They want to stone him to death. He tells the apostles that "Lazarus is dead." Appreciate what Thomas says in this passage: "Let us go along, to die *with him* [Jesus]." In a few days, during the hour of his Passion, they will leave him all alone.

2. Bethany is in mourning when Jesus finally arrives. Lazarus has been in the tomb four days. According to the customs of the East, there are many friends and acquaintances who have come to console Lazarus' two sisters around and about the house. From the moment Martha is told of Jesus' approaching arrival, she hurries off to meet him.

3. The conversation between Jesus and Martha:

"Lord, if you had been here, my brother would never have

died. Even now I am sure that God will give you whatever you ask of him." (Think over and appreciate the bitterness of Martha's sorrow but also her faith and hope.)

"Your brother will rise again" (his invitation to her to make an act of faith).

"I know he will rise again", Martha replied, "in the resurrection on the last day."

"I am the Resurrection and the life: whoever believes in me, though he should die, will come to life; and whoever is alive and believes in me will never die. Do you believe this?"

"Yes, Lord", she replied. "I have come to believe that you are the Messiah, the Son of God: he who was to come into the world."

Ponder over this conversation with what is the purest and strongest element of our faith in Jesus—with what is the most essential ingredient of faith.

4. Martha called Mary *secretly.* Jesus is still traveling undercover; it is best to be prudent!

Mary's act of faith.

When Jesus saw Mary's tears, *"He was troubled in spirit, moved by the deepest emotions."* And when they took him to see Lazarus' tomb, *Jesus began to weep.* See him weep, appreciate the emotion that brought tears to Jesus' eyes. "See how much he loved him."

Third Point: The Raising of Lazarus

Jesus begins by praying, and praying in a loud voice: "Father, I thank you for having heard me. I know that you always hear me, but I have said this for the sake of the crowd, that they may believe that you sent me." Thus Jesus is eager that no one misunderstand him: even the resurrection of Lazarus has to go beyond human considerations; it has to be "for the glory of God" and the faith of the spectators.

Jesus prays. He commands the dead man: "Lazarus, come out!"

Lazarus comes out from the tomb, tied hand and foot with linen strips and with his face wrapped in a cloth.

"Untie him and let him go free."

All is so simple, in so plain a style. Jesus has complete mastery over death.

Compare his attitude with the measures of the Pharisees and Sanhedrin: "The fact was, the chief priests planned to kill Lazarus too, because many Jews were going over to Jesus and believing in him on account of Lazarus" (John 12:10–11). The refusal to see so as not to believe . . . blindness and hate.

I will enter into a conversation with Christ our Lord about the content of this mystery. I will hear again the wonderful exchange between him and Martha, and I will make it my own conversation. I will talk with Lazarus. What gratitude must be his! What love he must have for him who gave back to him his life!

And us? And our baptism? And our hope for eternal life? Let us learn how to thank God.

I will end with the Our Father.

TWENTY-SECOND DAY

JESUS AT GRIPS WITH THE PHARISEES

The pages of the Gospel are filled with the Pharisees' hatred for Jesus. They are going to have him put to death. Among other passages, we shall meditate on verses 47 and 48 in chapter 19 of St. Luke's Gospel and on verses 37 and 38 in chapter 21, also from St. Luke's account.

Put yourself in the presence of God and make the preparatory prayer. Ask him to inspire you.

I will call to mind the *history* of the events that take place immediately before the Passion. Jesus teaches courageously in the temple each day. The Pharisees are present as well and are determined to have him put to death. But they do not know how to go about it, since the people, the crowds, are enthusiastic supporters of Jesus.

Composition of Place

The temple in Jerusalem: he is teaching here now, and the impression he makes on the doctors of the law is the same as it had been when he spoke to them here as a boy of twelve. He amazed them by his answers.

I will ask for *what I want and desire:* an intimate knowledge of Christ our Lord, who was made man for me, so that I can love him more and imitate him better.

First Point: Jesus Was Teaching during the Day in the Temple

What teaching! Truth came to light. At last the meaning of God's
written word is rediscovered, freed from the shackles and casu-
istry imposed by the Pharisees. The Mosaic law is accomplished,
fulfilled. The fount of life that is God-Love at this very moment is
again unsealed for all who thirst. The Living Water is within
reach of all, especially the humble and the little ones.

Jesus' teaching here before the doctors and the Pharisees is
simply a synthesis of all that he had been preaching about during
the past three years, namely, God's love for sinners:

"People do not pour new wine into old wineskins. . . . Nobody
sews a piece of unshrunken cloth on an old cloak" (Matt 9:16–17).

"The sabbath was made for man, not man for the sabbath"
(Mark 2:27).

"Is it lawful to work a cure on the sabbath?" (Matt 12:9).

He called to mind the frightening words of the prophets
against those who pay lip service to God but whose hearts are far
from God, and against those who equate sanctity with legalistic
observance and ritual practice alone (Matt 15).

And Jesus teaches with authority, not sparing his enemies. "If
you are really the Messiah, tell us so in plain words", they will
finally say to him. And unambiguously he will dare to affirm who
he is: "The Father and I are one. . . . I am the Son of God" (John
10:24–40).

His words go straight to the heart of the crowd: "At daybreak",
St. Luke reported, "all the people came to hear him in the temple"
(Luke 21:38).

*Second Point: The High Priests, the Scribes, and the Officials of the
People Looked for Some Way to Put Him to Death. But They Did
Not Know How to Lay Their Hands on Him Because All the People
Hung on His Every Word*

The Pharisees are totally obsessed by their hatred. We must feel
what this hatred is really like. The Pharisees stood for:

— the most demanding type of Jewish orthodoxy,

— a type of piety based on the strictest observance of the traditions of the ancients,

— the most exacting attention to all legal purities,

— the most unyielding zeal for anything concerning the law and its customs.

The word *Pharisee* means "separated". The members of this class are the "pure", the perfect—but their perfection is closed in on itself; they have eliminated spirit from their religion. "The father you spring from is the devil . . . he is a liar and the father of lies" (John 8:44). And again: "Woe to you scribes and Pharisees, you frauds! You are like whitewashed tombs, beautiful to look at on the outside but inside full of filth and dead men's bones" (Matt 23:27). And our Lord's great accusation against them: "You have taken away the key of knowledge. You yourselves have not gained access, yet you have stopped those who wish to enter" (Luke 11:52). The Good Shepherd defends his sheep, even his unfaithful sheep.

They finally decide to put Jesus to death. They pass this decision as a resolution at a meeting of the Sanhedrin (John 11:47–54). It was at this meeting that Caiaphas, the high priest, said, "Can you not see that it is better for you to have one man die for the people than to have the whole nation destroyed?"

But even though the resolution was passed, it was not executed because the people still "marveled at the appealing discourse that came from his lips" (Luke 4:22), just as they had when they heard him preach the Beatitudes.

Third Point: He Left the City to Spend the Night on the Mount of Olives

The Mount of Olives is quite close to the temple. Just the valley of the Kidron separates the two.

What a prelude this was to the coming night he would spend there in his agony!

Recounting what took place Holy Thursday night, St. Luke will say, "Then he went out and made his way, *as was his custom,* to the Mount of Olives" (Luke 22:39).

Consider in silence this prayer of Jesus. Discover his state of soul at this frightening time: during the day he was in the temple teaching; at night he was on the Mount of Olives resting, praying.

I will talk over these matters with Christ our Lord. Especially, I will ask him where I can find the true Life . . . and I will hear him answer me, "I am the Life."

I will end my meditation with the Our Father.

TWENTY-THIRD DAY

JESUS' TRIUMPHAL ENTRY
INTO JERUSALEM

Place yourself in the presence of God and make the prayer to begin the meditation.
Ask him to inspire you.

I will call to mind the *history* of the events as they are reported in St. Luke 19:29–41, St. Mark 11:1–10, or St. Matthew 21:1–9. Jesus is in the neighborhood of Bethany. He sends two of his disciples to pick up a donkey in a nearby town. He mounts the animal and rides into Jerusalem surrounded by an enthusiastic crowd of people who hail him as "he who comes in the name of the Lord".

Composition of Place

First, the road. It goes from Bethany up to Jerusalem (fifteen stadia, or a bit more than two miles). Then the narrow streets of Jerusalem.

I will ask for *what I want and desire.* Here it will be for the grace to penetrate the Heart of Jesus on that day of triumph to discover there at least a few of his sentiments in order to love and imitate him more.

First Point: The Prelude to the Triumphal Procession

Jesus is going up to Jerusalem. He passes Bethphage and Bethany. He knows his hour is approaching. The hate on the part of the Jews has reached its height. It is only right that the crowd recognize him for who he is before his death—this same crowd of men and women in a few days will be stirred up by the priests and Pharisees and will cry out to Pilate, "Crucify him!" . . . this same crowd to whom he preached the Beatitudes . . . the same crowd he has been teaching for the past three years and for whom he has performed many miracles. Doubtless in this same crowd there are people whom he pardoned or cured.

Jesus stops on his way and tells two of his disciples to go to the village ahead of them, where they will find a donkey. "If anyone should ask you, 'Why are you untying the beast?' say, 'The Master has need of it.'" The Master? Yes, he is recognized as such throughout the whole countryside. And the disciples found everything on their errand as he had said they would.

Second Point: Jesus Mounted the Colt, Seating Himself on the Cloaks the Disciples Had Spread out on Its Back

Matthew remarked that in doing this Jesus fulfilled what had been foretold by the prophets, particularly Zechariah (9:9): "Say to the daughter of Zion: look, your King is approaching, humble and riding on a donkey and on a colt, the foal of a beast of burden."

The exact text from Zechariah is even yet more beautiful and more significant: "See now, your King comes to you; he is victorious; he is triumphant", and it continues, "He will banish the chariots from Ephraim and horses from Jerusalem; the bow of war will be banished."

The Messiah King, as he was seen by the prophets, is humble and peaceful. He renounces the pomp and show of the kings of history and is satisfied to appear like the princes of Judah during the time of the patriarchs (Gen 49:11).

By fulfilling the prophecy of Zechariah, Jesus awakens in the soul of the people the comprehensive image of the Messiah and the messianic Kingdom. And the people understand. Soon they will greet Christ with words from Psalm 118: "Blessed is he who comes in the name of the Lord", and with the shout "Hosanna!" This is the acclamation proper to "the one who saves". And the people will perform an action spoken of by the Psalmist: "With branches in your hands draw up in procession" (Ps 118:27).

Such is the true meaning of Christ our Lord's messianic entry into Jerusalem. It shows us what his intention was in coming into the city the way he did. It tells us that even on this day of his triumph, he is not about to take on the attitude of a proud ruler or a triumphant warlord. He is "the just man"; he is "the humble man"; he comes to rescue man from his Luciferlike pride.

Third Point: The Triumphant Procession

1. The people spread their cloaks along the road as he passes. They cut branches from the trees and join in the triumphal procession.

2. As the cortège makes its way past the Mount of Olives and then approaches Jerusalem, the crowd breaks out in cries: "Hosanna! Blessed is he who comes in the name of the Lord! Blessed is the reign of our father David to come! Hosanna in the highest!"

3. A few Pharisees mixed in with the crowd and advised Jesus, "Master, rebuke your disciples!" And Jesus responded, "If they were to keep silence, I tell you the very stones would cry out."

4. Soon all of Jerusalem is in commotion. Jesus makes his way to the temple. The blind and the lame are there. He cures them. The scribes and Pharisees ask him if he hears what the children are crying out within the temple precincts—"Hosanna to the Son of David"—and if he does, to make them stop. "Of course I hear them", he answers. "Did you never read this: 'From the speech of infants and children you have framed a hymn of praise'?"

I will converse with Christ about these events. I will add my own praises to the acclamations of the crowd. Especially, I will try to penetrate the sentiments of his heart: before this crowd . . . before Jerusalem . . . as he progresses along the streets, which soon will witness a procession of a different type.

I will end my contemplation with the Our Father.

THIRD WEEK

The hour is at hand,
"his hour".
In the life of Christ our Lord here on this earth,
this is the hour for which he came
into the world.

The Passion
is a historic event
and also a mystery of love.

It is renewed in the Church
and made accessible to each of us
in the sacrifice of the Mass.

THE LAST SUPPER

Everything is love in this Third Week of the Exercises; it is a love that is excessive, infinite, really altogether too much for our understanding. This is why we must accept this revelation from the heart of God and let ourselves be open to the mysteries of the Passion and death of Jesus with utmost simplicity. This comes from nothing less than complete faith in God's goodness and power. Only God can love us—can love me—to the point of suffering and dying for us—for me—in such a way.

Place yourself in God's presence and make the preparatory prayer.
Ask him to inspire you.

I will call to mind the *history* of the mystery. Christ our Lord sent two apostles from Bethany to Jerusalem to prepare the Passover meal. Later he and the other apostles came up to join the two. After eating the paschal lamb according to the rituals prescribed by Moses, he washed the apostles' feet, instituted the Holy Eucharist, and for a long time spoke with his apostles "as one friend to another".

Composition of Place

I will see the road that leads from Bethany up to Jerusalem. Then I will imagine the Cenacle, the place where the Last Supper takes place: "an upstairs room," St. Mark writes, "spacious, furnished, and all in order" (Mark 14:15).

I will ask for *what I want and desire.* Here it is sorrow, compassion, shame, because the Lord is going to his Passion for my sins.

First Point: The Last Supper

I look at Jesus. He is totally aware of the symbolism of the Passover in the old law; it was simply the prefiguration of what will happen to him tonight and tomorrow. The final hour for the world has come. God's plan, wrought from pure goodness and love, "the plan he was pleased to decree in Christ", is about to be accomplished (Eph 1:9). Man will again "share in the glorious freedom of the children of God" (Rom 8:21). The world will be reconciled with God and with itself. The New Covenant will be entered into and will last forever.

Let us admire the carefulness of Christ our Lord to fulfill the Scriptures and tie in the Old Testament with the New.

Let us contemplate and feel deeply in ourselves his tremendous desire: "I have greatly desired to eat this Passover with you before I suffer" (Luke 22:15). What love for his Father and for us! Oh, Eucharist!

He speaks of the Kingdom of God, his Kingdom: "I tell you I shall not eat the Passover again until it is fulfilled in the Kingdom of God. . . . I shall not drink of the fruit of the vine until the coming of the reign of God" (Luke 22:16–17).

Second Point: The Washing of the Feet

A gesture of the greatest significance because of the solemnity of the moment.

1. The Church of Jesus Christ will be a hierarchical Church, but he gives an unprecedented meaning to hierarchy, to authority:

The apostles are caught up in a dispute about the Kingdom of heaven: "An argument also began between them about who should be reckoned the greatest."

Jesus said, "No, the greatest among you must behave as if he were the youngest, the leader as if he were the one who serves" (Luke 22:24–26).

"Anyone among you who aspires to greatness must serve the rest" (Mark 10:43).

"And whoever wants to rank first among you must serve the needs of all" (Matt 20:27).

He himself has given the example: "Such is the case with the Son of Man who has come not to be served by others but to serve, to give his own life as a ransom for many" (Matt 20:28).

Now he joins what he says with what he does: "He rose from the meal and took off his cloak. He picked up the towel and tied it around himself. Then he poured water into a basin and began to wash his disciples' feet and dry them with the towel he had around him" (John 13:4-5).

What a revolution in the concept of a community and the role played by its chief and leader!

2. The conversation between Judas and Peter:

Yes, Jesus has washed the feet of Judas. With what tenderness and consideration! He has already stated on a number of occasions that he was aware of Judas' intentions. But the traitor set his face against him. Finally, Jesus told him, "Be quick about what you are to do", and Judas left. In reporting the scene St. John uses an astounding expression: "It was night". Night!—outside, or in the heart of the traitor (John 13:17-30)?

Jesus also washes the feet of Peter. At first Peter refuses: "Never! You shall never wash my feet." Jesus had to convince him with a decisive argument: "If I do not wash you, you can have no share *with me.*" (*Mecum!*) And Peter gives the response of the *insignes:* "Well, then, Lord, not only my feet but my hands and my head as well!" (John 13:6-8). To be *with Jesus* one must be ready to be with him all the way. Generous Peter is, but not sinless!

Third Point: Jesus Institutes the Eucharist and the Priesthood

1. Let us reread the admirable account of what takes place next either in 1 Corinthians 11:17-30, to which we should add

1 Corinthians 10:16–17, or in one of the Synoptics (Luke 22; Mark 14; Matt 26)—or the words of the canons in our missal.

In order to understand the correct and literal sense of the Eucharist, it would be good to reread chapter 6 in St. John's Gospel: "I am the bread of life. No one who comes to me will ever hunger; no one who believes in me will ever thirst. . . . It is my Father's will that whoever sees the Son and believes in him should have eternal life and that I should raise that person up on the Last Day . . . and the bread I shall give is my flesh, for the life of the world. . . . Whoever eats my flesh and drinks my blood lives in me, and I live in that person." Now listen to those who hear him on this occasion murmur, see them walking away . . . and repeat with St. Peter, "Lord, to whom shall we go? You have the message of eternal life, and we believe."

2. The whole structural meaning of the Old Testament is summed up here (Heb 8 to 10). The priesthood comes into being.

3. Let us meditate with feeling on John's expression: "He had loved his own in the world and would show his love for them to the end" (John 13:1). *"In finem dilexit eos"*: He loved them to the end, to the extremity of his infinite love. This is how he loved me: *Dilexit me.*

In finem: to the end.
— Here is where the Incarnation and the thematic development of his love reach their fulfillment.
— Here is where the self-abasement of Christ our Lord is realized. The eucharistic state!
— Here the redemption is accomplished because through the Eucharist Christ promises to go to the limits of the Passion, all the way to the Resurrection.
— Here is fulfilled the Mosaic law and here begins (reaches its completion) the new law. Jesus will soon begin his "last discourse" with the new commandment of fraternal charity, and he will develop God's new plan, the "restored" plan *"mirabilis reformasti"*.

— Here the *"sint unum"* — that they may be one — of the priestly prayer reaches completion. Through the Eucharist the Church is already established.

And everything the Eucharist means for Christ, it means for the priest.

How the Divinity hides itself. "Oh, hidden God, I adore you!"

I will converse with Christ our Lord. Many things I have to talk to him about here: adoration, faith, thanksgiving. May what he asked for in his "last discourse" and his "sacerdotal prayer" be realized through me.

I will end my contemplation with the Our Father. What meaning the Lord's prayer takes on here, in the upper room, this evening!

THE AGONY IN THE GARDEN

Every event that takes place during the Passion actually encompasses all the other events. For this reason let us follow more closely than ever before St. Ignatius' advice: "I will remain quietly meditating upon the point in which I have found what I desire, without any eagerness to go on until I have been satisfied."

Place yourself in the presence of God and make the prayer beginning the meditation.
Ask him to inspire you.

I will recall first of all the *history* of what is covered in this meditation. Christ our Lord went down from Mount Zion (where he had eaten the Last Supper with his twelve apostles) toward the Valley of Jehoshaphat, and then up toward the Garden of Olives. He leaves eight of the apostles just outside the Garden; the remaining three—Peter, James, and John—he brings with him into the Garden. Then, leaving these three, he goes more deeply into the olive groves, where he begins to pray. During his prayer his sweat becomes like drops of blood. After having prayed three times to his Father, he wakes up the three disciples. His enemies make their appearance, Judas leading them on. Judas gives him a kiss of peace. St. Peter cuts off the ear of Malchus, and Jesus heals the wound. They arrest him as if he were a bandit. Next they drag him down to the valley and then up the opposite hill to Jerusalem and to the house of Annas.

Composition of Place

See the two roads. The first is the short road going from Mount Zion down to the valley of Jehoshaphat. From the valley rise up two hills. On the slopes of the eastern one is the Mount of Olives. It faces the western hill, where Mount Zion is located and where, behind, the walls of Jerusalem are visible. Then there is the road from the walls to the house of Annas.

I will ask for *what I want and desire*. Here it is proper to ask for sorrow with Christ in sorrow, anguish with Christ in anguish, interior grief because of the great sufferings Christ endures for me.

First Point: What Is at Stake in the Struggle of Christ Our Lord

What is at stake is his "glorious freedom as a Son of God", the filial adherence of his will to the will of the Father, his love, his total and definitive Yes to the Father.

Here Jesus is faced with the essential act that must be accomplished to complete the Father's plan of love, the plan the prophets prophesied without fully understanding its meaning: "They investigated the times and the circumstances that the Spirit of Christ within them was pointing to, for he predicted the sufferings destined for Christ and the glories that would follow" (1 Pet 1:11). This is the profound mystery the angels watched in astonishment.

Jesus is alone during his struggle. When he arrived in Gethsemane, he told his eight apostles, "Stay here while I go over there to pray". A little later he said to Peter, James, and John, "Wait here and stay awake with me" (Matt 26:37–39). A terrible sense of loneliness. He will scarcely be able to stand it; three times he will return to those who were supposed to watch with him . . . they slept . . . yes, indeed, he is alone, completely alone!

He sees before him the world of sin, and he sees also divine love, misunderstood and scorned . . . sins of every age . . . sins of every person. Or better: he sees sinful human nature, torn away from the Father, enslaved to the "Prince of Darkness".

He feels the malice, the total perversity of this sin in the world—this evil that we cannot grasp with our reason and that goes far beyond our understanding—but he is able to measure it against the Father's overabundant love because he has always known the heart of the Father.

He knows that only an excessive redemption (his Passion) or an excessive punishment (hell) could correspond to his Father's excessive love. He was caught up in this awesome dilemma; and now the hour has come for him to decide, to choose once and for all. Or rather, as St. Paul says, because he is the Yes to all the Father's promises, the hour is come for him to ratify his mission (1 Cor 1:20).

"My heart is nearly broken with sorrow" (Matt 26:38). He was afraid. Fright and dejection pour into his soul. Feel, ponder, and mull over this "desolation" of the Son of God. Indeed, with the exception of sin itself, he was truly clothed "in the same sinful flesh" as ourselves (Rom 8:3).

And the drama of his choice was that it had repercussions throughout his flesh.

Even to the point that he sweat blood: "And his sweat became like drops of blood falling to the ground" (Luke 22:44). "This supposes", comments St. Ignatius, "that his garments were saturated with blood."

During this agony he is tempted: tempted as he was before by Satan in the desert, tempted to give up, to forget it all. "*Abba* [O Father], you have the power to do all things. Take this cup away from me!" (Mark 14:36). Contemplate to what extent Jesus must be dejected, oppressed, to let such words escape from his filial lips. What disgust, what bitterness! We should observe that he did not revolt against his Father's will; he simply desired that that will would change.

At this point of his temptation, one word would change everything. He had cried out, "*Abba* [O Father]!" This is not a cry of revolt or hopeless resignation; it is the cry of a son, a cry of confidence in the Father at the height of his suffering, a cry that is already acceptance. In that word *Abba* there is already contained all of the *"non mea voluntas, sed tua fiat"*, that is, all of the meaning contained in the prayer: "But let it be as you would have it, not as I."

Three times he came back to see his apostles. They were sleeping. Three times he returned to his place of prayer: "Going back again, he began to pray in the same words" (Mark 14:39); "Father, if it is your will, take this cup from me; yet not my will but yours be done" (Luke 22:42).

Love came out the victor from this agony of Christ. "Liberty" triumphed. "The Father and I are one" of the priestly prayer is affirmed here in the Person of Christ our Lord. In him our sinful flesh becomes a flesh of obedience and filial fidelity.

Second Point: Jesus' Prayer

This prayer of Jesus at Gethsemane can be considered as the pattern for prayer, the model of all prayer, the prayer that goes beyond all methods.

1. Indeed, to some extent the drama of the redemption must always be operative at the heart of every prayer: our own personal drama, inseparable from who we are, but which we must live with Jesus Christ.

Let us pay particular attention to what St. Luke says when Jesus leaves the upper room on Holy Thursday night: "He then left to make his way *as usual* to the Mount of Olives, with his disciples following" (Luke 22:39). His agony this night had been preceded by other "agonies".

2. In this drama of prayer we are accompanied by our temptations and contradictions, by our outbursts of generosity and our moments of selfishness, by our acts of submission and our movements of revolt, by our times of peace and our moments of distress. Just like Jesus, who both *desired* this hour and had a *disgust* and a *horror* of it, let us not be surprised by the wavering of our own will. It is part of the work of redemption. A person can be

"desolate and tempted to run off" and at the same time love and say Yes to our Father.

3. This personal drama has to play itself out in our prayer. The circumstances of who we are, what we do, and what is in store for us in the future (our activities, sufferings, joys, failures, etc.)—all of these we have to bear. At the same time, we bear them all in our personal conscience and in our conscience as Christians; that is, we bear all of these as men who participate with Christ in the redemption of the world.

4. *Father*—this is the word that saves all—which necessarily is *"Ita, Pater"* (Yes, Father). The importance and the beauty in our lives of the prayer the Our Father . . . its place at the heart of our deepest being . . . it is here at Gethsemane that Jesus teaches us to say this prayer.

5. Let us be humble, as Jesus was humble, in this combat that is our prayer. He, the Son of God, calls for and accepts the comfort of the angel. The angel is the sign of the love of the Father. Let us look for and accept everything that can assist us in our prayer. Such is the prayer of the poor man! Such is the prayer of the publican! Such is the prayer of the Canaanite woman!

6. If our prayer is a redemptive prayer, we should not be surprised if it wanders here and there and that we are always repeating the same words. At Gethsemane Jesus comes and goes; he looks for support does not find it, but, as St. Mark tells us, "Going back again he began to pray in the same words" (14:39). A love without words . . . a prayer more real than the most beautiful formulas ever composed.

7. Despite his personal agony, Jesus thinks of others, of his apostles: "Be on guard and pray that you may not undergo the test" (Matt 26:41). "And lead us not into temptation."

8. Savor the contrast of the tragic prayer at Gethsemane with the energetic "Get up! Let us be on our way!" that he says as Judas and the cohort come into the Garden (Matt 26:46). Strength: that

is what comes from redemptive prayer. The Virgin Mary, the coredemptrix, *stood* near the Cross of Jesus (John 19:25).

Third Point: The Apostles Run Off

The sequel to all of the events that occurred up to the time of his capture takes place before the Passion, when his body is mutilated. It comes about now in the passion that rips apart his human heart, that is, when his own ran off abandoning him, forsaking him.

"With that, all deserted him and fled", reports St. Mark (14:50). Think about how sad that word *all* is.

All, even Peter, the fighter.

All, even John, "the disciple whom Jesus loved".

All? No, over there is his Mother. She shows compassion for him. But for him, his Mother's compassion means an increase of suffering.

All? No, Judas is there, too. He gives him the only sign of friendship this night—a kiss. But this particular kiss is the sign of treason. Jesus does not shirk from Judas' kiss, but think about how bitter it is for him. Consider the infinite sadness in his complaint: "*Friend,* do what you are here for!" (Matt 26:50).

I will close my contemplation by *conversing about these matters* with Christ our Lord, who goes to his Passion for my sins: "He poured out for you every drop of his blood" (Pascal). After watching Peter flee and John run off, dare I pose here the questions I asked myself in the Colloquy of Mercy: "What will I do for Christ? What should I do for Christ?" After seeing the kiss of friendship perverted—"Friend, a kiss . . . ?"—dare I talk with him "as one friend to another"?

In my confusion I will catch up with Peter: Peter "following him from afar" and who will deny him, but who will immediately weep over his treachery. This then is the irony of that grace I have prayed for during the Second Week: "So that I may imitate him better and follow him more closely". On this Holy Thursday evening in the company of Peter I feel I have the companionship I need. I am ... far off; but I do follow him, and that in itself is already something!

Then I will meet up with our Lady and ask her for her heart, her tears, to *com pati,* to "suffer with" Jesus in his distress as he goes to his Passion.

I will conclude with the Our Father.

Twenty-Sixth Day

THE VIA DOLOROSA:
JESUS AT THE HOUSE OF CAIAPHAS
AND BEFORE THE SANHEDRIN

Place yourself in the presence of God and make the prayer that begins the meditation.
Ask him to inspire you.

I will call to mind the *history* of the events. Jesus' hands are bound, and he is dragged from the Garden of Olives to the house of Annas (the father-in-law of the High Priest Caiaphas). But Annas sends him back to Caiaphas (John 18:24). Peter is there and denies his Master three times. Meanwhile, until daybreak, when the Sanhedrin will meet, Jesus is insulted, taunted, and slapped by his guards. Morning arrives, and the elders of the people, the chief priests, and the scribes meet together in the council of the Sanhedrin. They condemn Jesus to death. Judas, in despair, hangs himself. After passing sentence, Caiaphas has him sent to Pilate, the Roman governor, who alone has the power to pronounce the death penalty.

Composition of Place

I will see the house of the High Priest Caiaphas with its courtyard where his retainers are warming their hands and where Peter comes and sits down ... with its guardhouse where Jesus is manhandled, brutalized ... and with its grand hall where the Sanhedrin meets and where Jesus is condemned for having said he is the "Son of God".

176

I will ask for *what I want and desire.* Here it will be sorrow with Christ in sorrow, anguish with Christ in anguish, interior grief for so much suffering that Christ endures for me.

First Point: Peter's Triple Denial

1. I am in the inner court of Caiaphas' house. In one corner is Jesus. He is all tied up and used by the guards as if he were something to spit at. They also beat him up and taunt him. Then, covering his eyes, they strike him: "Prophesy! Who struck you?" In another corner a fire is burning. Servants and soldiers are sitting around it warming their hands. Peter comes up, and he sits down, too. He is full of remorse for having run off when Jesus was arrested. Follow the events as they are presented by St. Mark (14:54–73).

2. The atmosphere around the fire lends itself to easy conversation: "You too were with Jesus of Nazareth." Peter denies it: "I do not even know the man you are talking about!" What irony!

3. Then Jesus turns and looks at Peter (Luke 22:61). Contemplate that look. Peter gets up and leaves. He cries bitterly. Reflect on Peter's tears.

Second Point: Jesus before Caiaphas and the Sanhedrin

1. The Sanhedrin looked for testimony to bring against Jesus. But the witnesses succeeded only in contradicting themselves. At last, one of them recalled that Jesus had said, "I shall destroy this temple made by human hands, and in three days I will construct another not made by human hands" (see Mark 14:58).

2. Finally, the high priest asked him, "Are you the Messiah, the Son of the Blessed One?" And Jesus answered, "I am, and you will see the Son of Man seated at the right hand of the Power and coming with the clouds of heaven."

3. The high priest tore his robes and said, "What further need

do we have of witnesses? You have heard the blasphemy. What is your verdict?" And they all condemned him to death (Mark 14:63–64).

Third Point: Judas

1. Then Judas, seeing that Jesus was condemned, repented. Think about the despair contained in that repentance.

2. He brought back the thirty pieces of silver, the price of his treasonous act. The chief priests and elders refused to accept it. What a complicated predicament the traitor has created for himself! Does this make him repent? Does he now turn interiorly toward Jesus? Or does he despair?

3. Judas throws the thirty pieces of silver on the temple floor and then goes out and hangs himself.

Consider and try to appreciate the traitor's loss of hope; such a heavy weight brooded over his soul. What a difference between his attitude and that of Peter!

I will converse with Christ our Lord, offended and condemned for my sins. I will adore him. I will say to him what the priest prays just before Communion at Mass: "Never let me be parted from you." I will ask him that, if ever I should be so evil as to betray him, I may shed the tears of Peter rather than give in to the despair of Judas.

I will end the meditation with the Our Father.

TWENTY–SEVENTH DAY

THE VIA DOLOROSA:
FROM PILATE'S PRAETORIUM TO CALVARY

What happens here is beyond all words. Each person will follow where grace bids him to go so as "to enter" intimately into the mystery of Christ's death.

Here are *three suggestions.* The retreatant may want to select one or another among them as he desires.

1. *Read over slowly,* peacefully, lovingly—with the attitude one has when he assists at the Mass or reads the office of Good Friday—*the whole Passion* from one of the four evangelists.

St. Ignatius would have approved using the *lexio divina* here. He gives the following advice to the retreatant who "wishes to spend more time on the Passion": "When he finishes the Passion [that is, taking mystery after mystery for the subject of his contemplation], he may devote one whole day to the consideration of the first half of the Passion and a second day to the other half and a third day to the whole Passion."

2. Make a lengthy, deeply contemplative *Way of the Cross.* It should be very personal. See the events clearly as they are, in their tragic reality.

3. Listen to, ponder over, reflect upon the *Seven Words of Christ on the Cross:*

— "Father, forgive them; they do not know what they are doing."
— "Today you will be *with me* in paradise."

— "Woman, there is your son. This is your mother."
— "My God, my God, why have you forsaken me?"
— "I am thirsty."
— "Now it is finished."
— "Father, into your hands I commend my spirit."

Whatever choice one would make, he could *enhance the reality of the contemplation* by choosing one or more of these options:

— Reading St. Paul's account of the gradual self-abasement of the Word of God (Phil 2:6–11).
— reflecting on the passage from Galatians (2:20) about the "Son of God, who loved me and gave himself for me".
— Renewing the Colloquy of Mercy (see pp. 74–77).
— Reconsidering the Call of the King and the Two Standards;
— Implementing in my day-to-day attitudes the recommendations St. Ignatius gives to those making the Third Week:

— "To consider what Christ our Lord suffers in his human nature; to do all in my power to suffer and be sad for him".
— "To consider how the Divinity hides itself; for example, it could annihilate its enemies, yet it does not do so but leaves the most sacred humanity to endure so many cruel sufferings."
— "To consider how our Lord suffers so much for my sins and what I ought to do and to suffer for him".

This whole contemplation ought to be a *conversation,* a friendly colloquy with my Savior, and most especially it should be a "simple looking at", a "pure consideration". The Passion makes its appeal to faith and the heart, not to words. It is a mystery of love before which I simply allow myself to be so that, imperceptibly and gradually, I can be drawn more deeply into its depths.

I will again end my prayer with the Our Father—this time at the foot of the Cross where the words take on an extraordinary meaning. I shall also repeat word by word the prayer Soul of Christ (*Anima Christi*).

TWENTY-EIGHTH DAY

THE SOLITUDE OF OUR LADY

As I complete these contemplations on the great mystery of the Passion of Christ our Lord, I shall consider, by way of a repetition, the solitude experienced by our Lady on Good Friday evening and during the course of the following day. Many people have used this "Holy Saturday spirituality" as a way to God. The ancient Fathers recommended our reminding God of Jesus and what he did for each and all of us as an excellent method of prayer.

Place yourself in the presence of God and make the prayer beginning the contemplation.
Ask him to inspire you.

I will call to mind the *history* of the events. Our Lady was present with Jesus on his way to Calvary. She stood near the Cross. Jesus told his Mother that John was now her son while giving his beloved disciple his Mother. There was the descent from the Cross. Afterward Jesus was placed in the tomb. Then she went home with John. Mary is the most perfect model of the *"Mecum"*, that is, the "with me"; she indeed is the one who had "compassion", "suffered with", her Son. In the eyes of the crowd who put him to death, she was the mother of "the Imposter", the mother of the one who was condemned. And in the eyes of God?

181

Composition of Place

In a little private room in the place where John was housed.

I will ask for *what I want and desire.* Here it will be a heart to "empathize", that is, to "feel within" me what Jesus Christ feels.

First Point: The Solitude of Our Lady between the Passion and the Resurrection

1. The cause for this terrible solitude: "he" is no longer here:

He, her Son! She watched over him as a small baby. Then there was Bethlehem . . . Nazareth . . . his farewell to her before beginning his public life . . . Cana. All of these things she "kept in her heart", and particularly those events she witnessed during the Passion.

She contemplates "the sufferings, pains, and anguish that Christ our Lord endured from the time of his birth down to Calvary", just as St. Ignatius asks us to consider them.

The sword of sorrow, predicted by Simeon, pierced her soul. She is the one who knows who Jesus truly is because she is the one who lives out fully the drama of our redemption. And she reconciles this drama perfectly within her own soul. Like Jesus during his agony in the Garden, her response is also, "Yes, Father."

2. Even though full of sorrow, hers was a faith-filled, hope-filled solitude:

Stabat Mater: Mary *stood* beneath the Cross, her faith intact.

Her faith never knew the fluctuation and hesitations of the faith of the apostles.

Her Son no longer suffers. The pain-filled phase of the redemption is finished: "For your faithful people life is changed, not ended", as the Preface of the Mass of the Dead tells us.

She knows the Resurrection is certain and that it is near. She remembers the words of Jesus announcing his Resurrection—and that "that imposter while he was still alive made the claim, 'After three days I will rise'" (Matt 27:63). And that he will rebuild the temple (of his body) in three days.

She further recalled, "And I—once I am lifted up from earth—will draw all men to myself" (John 12:32). Yes, that day was already dawning. It began at Calvary: there were the good thief, the centurion, and those who "went home beating their breasts" (Luke 23:48). The realization of all of this did not stave off her grief as a mother, yet the joy of charity gave some perspective to her sorrow.

It was because of this certitude that her anguish, even though not diminished, was nevertheless appeased. Spend a long time reflecting on our Lady's serenity, on this quiet peace.

3. Her solitude, however, was filled up by the presence of the the Holy Trinity:

Her unity with the Trinity was, of course, never interrupted. But today that unity is more centered, more intense. The "beneficent plan" of the Father is realized. The Annunciation is accomplished: "I am the servant of the Lord. Let it be done to me as you say" (Luke 1:38). How far-reaching are certain words in the world's destiny!

The Son. Think about how he said, "My Mother"! It was with the same resonance, the same tenderness that he said, "My Father", that is, in the Holy Spirit. Without her the redemption would have been impossible. Because of her Immaculate Conception she benefited in an exceptional way in the Son's redemption, and therefore he rejoiced in her, the first of his redeemed.

The Holy Spirit, to whom she was always perfectly disposed. He now wants her to assist in his future enterprise, that is, in creating the Church, in being the soul of his soul.

Spend a long time savoring this solitude, this silence, this simplicity of our Lady. How beautiful, how wonderful it is!

Second Point: Our Lady's Solitude Is Open to the Apostles Who Return

Because they too are "alone". But their loneliness is of a completely different type from Mary's solitude. Their solitude is the aloneness of the sinner, of him "who would deserve to be reprimanded and considered fainthearted", as we considered in the meditation of the call of the King. The solitude of those like the disciples on their way to Emmaus, "who had hoped", and who were disappointed by the events that had taken place, and who had seen their dreams shattered. The solitude of sterility and desolation. How bitter!

Mary welcomes John. She was living where he was lodged. He had been with her at Calvary: "Woman, there is your son" (John 19:26). By privileged title, from that moment on, he is her son. He mourns the death of a friend, and what a Friend . . . a Brother in Mary!

She welcomes the turncoat Peter. She reminds him: "You are Peter, and on this rock, he will build his Church. . . . He had predicted that you would deny him three times before the cock crowed, but once converted, you would strengthen your brothers . . . . Be up and about now, Peter. The time has come for you to give them courage." She taught him humility, the beautiful, holy by-product of sin. It was from Mary that Peter learned to rely no longer on himself ("Peter, do you love me?") but on Jesus alone, who knew him and who would give him confidence ("Lord, you know that I love you").

She welcomes the other apostles. They had believed themselves so strong, and yet they all ran off, all of them. Now, one by one, they return. She would love to welcome even Judas, to pardon him, and to remind him of the many, many times he had seen her Son extend pardon to others. She would tell him, "He loves you, and he gave himself up for you. *Dilexit te.*" And she would also say, "The one who was pardoned the most is the one who is loved the most."

Undoubtedly Mary Magdalen also came to see our Lady. And Martha, and Mary of Bethany. And Lazarus, whom Jesus raised from the dead.

With courtesy and affection she communicated to all of these her peace, her faith, and her hope. She initiates the role of "the comforter", a role that the resurrected Jesus will so magnificently exercise. It is a role that is not by any means mere playacting but one in which the person gives only what he truly "has" and what he really "is".

Rest awhile in a corner of that room, listening, watching, contemplating, admiring.

Third Point: The Church Is Already Begun in the Very Heart of Christ's Failure

Yes, that is so, thanks to this woman full of grief but with her faith intact.

It is with faith-filled grief that she gathers together Jesus' friends, one after the other. On Easter morning the regroupment will be complete. It is a sparse and humble band—like the "remnant of Israel" of old, like so many grains of wheat buried in the ground, where the "power of God" will have them sprout forth a harvest.

This will be the group associated with the Resurrection, ascension, and Pentecost, the very first Christian community. And so the Church is planted in the world, a group of true friends of Jesus who *believe* in his Resurrection!

And here is an admirable thing to reflect upon: at the same time that she renounces her precious solitude to give birth to the Church, our Lady discovers another solitude, another silence *in* the Church: "Peter, it is you who will command, govern, and rule. You are Peter." The Acts of the Apostles will mention her again, but very seldom. Nothing about the risen Jesus' apparition to his Mother, nothing about her life, nothing about her death. In Christian Tradition there will be two places of the "Dormition of the Virgin", one at Jerusalem, the other at Ephesus. Silence, solitude, but she is at the very heart of the living Church.

After fulfilling her historic role as Redemptrix, she will begin here her role as Mediatrix, the Mother of every Christian.

I also will converse with our Lady, begging her to pardon me for having betrayed her Son, confiding to her, in spite of my wretchedness, that I still desire to love and to imitate her Son: "Hail, Mother of mercy"; "Pray for us sinners!"

I will end my prayer with the Our Father.

FOURTH WEEK

In the Father's love
with the resurrected Jesus,
"the Head of the body that is the Church".

THE RESURRECTION AND THE APPARITIONS OF THE RISEN CHRIST

First of all, here are a few recommendations St. Ignatius gives us to create the atmosphere of the Fourth Week.

"As soon as I awaken, I shall place before my mind the scene I am about to contemplate; I shall seek to stir up in myself the joy and happiness of Christ our Lord, and I shall endeavor to find enjoyment in thinking about it."

"I will think about subjects that stimulate happiness, cheerfulness, and spiritual joy, such as the glory of heaven."

"I shall make use of the sunshine of the day, of the pleasures of the season, etc., insofar as my soul esteems that all of these things may help it rejoice in its Creator and in its Redeemer."

Place yourself in God's presence and make the prayer that begins the meditation.
Ask him to inspire you.

I will call to mind the *history* of the events in this mystery. The exact account of the event itself is found nowhere in the Gospels. Where we have the proof of the Resurrection are in the empty tomb, in the unquestionable testimony of the holy women who went to the sepulchre early in the morning carrying spices, and in the experience of Peter and John. In addition to these there were the apparitions of the risen Christ during the course of the next forty days that would give the Resurrection its true significance (see St. Paul's stated case in I Cor 15:1–11).

Composition of Place

The tomb in the Church of the Holy Sepulchre at Jerusalem or before some tomb in the countryside. In front of it there is a massive, heavy, round rock that is used to seal the entrance.

I will ask for *what I want and desire*. Here it is the grace of experiencing intense gladness and joy because of the great glory and joy of Christ our Lord.

During the course of the Fourth Week St. Ignatius advises us:

1. To consider how the Divinity, which seemed to hide itself during the Passion, now appears and reveals itself so wonderfully in the holy Resurrection.

2. To spend some time admiring the role of consoler that Christ our Lord plays. He acts just like ordinary friends do when they want to console one another: "He loved me."

First Point: The Empty Tomb

"Jesus of Nazareth is not here, for he has risen, as he said he would" (Matt 28:6).

Let us take our place among the group of apostles and disciples who cluster about our Lady on Easter morning. Most probably they are at John's house. (We are not going to try to orchestrate the various apparitions according to when and where they took place because the Gospel accounts offer no such arrangement. Rather, what we are going to do for the most part is follow the account found in John's Gospel [20:1–10], because John is an *exact* witness, telling us what he *saw*. His witness is supported by Luke [24:12], who in turn received his account from Peter, another *witness* to the events.)

In the morning, "while it was still dark", the women carrying their spices left for the tomb of Christ. They did not perform these burial rites the day before because they observed the sabbath as a day of rest. These women were Mary Magdalen, Joanna, and Mary the mother of James. Let us accompany them as they make their way along the road. "Who will roll back the stone for us from the entrance to the tomb?" (Mark 16:3). But when they arrive at their destination they find the stone rolled aside and the tomb opened and empty.

Mary Magdalen runs off to alert Peter and "the other disciple (the one Jesus loved)". She reports, "The Lord has been taken from the tomb! We do not know where they have put him."

However, the other women, who had stayed close by the sepulchre, entered the tomb, where they saw "a young man" (according to Mark and Matthew, and "two young men", according to Luke) dressed in white who said to them, "There is no need to be so amazed.... Why do you search for the Living One among the dead? You are looking for Jesus of Nazareth; he has been raised up. Remember what he said to you while he was still in Galilee—that the Son of Man must be delivered into the hands of sinful men and be crucified and on the third day rise again.... See, here is the place where they laid him" (Luke 24:5–7; Mark 16:6). The women made their way out of the tomb bewildered and trembling because "they were frightened out of their wits" (Mark 16:8).

When Peter learns the news from Mary Magdalen, he takes John with him and runs off to the sepulchre. John is the first to arrive but does not enter the tomb. Peter arrives and goes in. There he sees the burial wrappings and the piece of cloth that had covered the face and head of the dead Jesus. He saw "the piece of cloth that had covered the head not lying with the wrappings, but rolled up in a place by itself" (John 20:7). Then John enters the tomb: "He saw and believed." The two disciples return home. Finally, sometime during the day Jesus appears to Peter (Luke 24:34).

Mary Magdalen had remained in the vicinity of the tomb. Now she is crying. Jesus appears to her: "Woman, why are you weeping? Who is it that you are looking for?" She takes him for the gardener and says, "Sir, if you are the one who carried him off, tell me where you have put him, and I will go and remove him" . . . "Maryam" . . . "Rabbouni" (John 20:11–19).

What confusion there is now among his faithful followers in Jerusalem! Joy is mixed with apprehension! What is the meaning of all of this? We get some inkling of the uneasiness in the words of the disciples who were making their way to Emmaus on that Sunday afternoon: "Some of the women of our group have just brought us some astonishing news", they say. "They were at the tomb before dawn and failed to find his body but returned with the tale that they had seen a vision of angels who declared he was alive. Some of our number went to the tomb and found it to be just as the women said, but they did not see him" (Luke 24:22–24). The confusion becomes more widespread throughout Jerusalem. The Sanhedrin order the men guarding the tomb to get the word around that the disciples have stolen the body.

Relive this Easter morning. Appreciate the fear of Jesus' friends and their progressive growth in faith, hope, and love.

Second Point: The Resurrection and Christian Faith

Reread St. Paul's beautiful text in I Corinthians 15:12–26.

The totality of our Christian belief rests on our faith in the Resurrection of Jesus: "If Christ has not been raised, our preaching is void of content, and your faith is empty, too. . . . If our hopes in Christ are limited to this life only, we are the most pitiable of men."

When the apostles first went out to preach the Gospel message, they made the death and Resurrection of Jesus the pivotal point of their message (the Kerygma). Read Peter's five discourses (Acts 2, 3, 10, etc.) and Paul's sermon in Acts 13.

It is in the Resurrection that we find the essence of our Faith, the epicenter of the Creed. One day we too shall rise with a body similar to that of the risen Christ (see I Cor 15:35–38).

Third Point: The Resurrection and Christian Life

Reread once more the text describing "the kenosis" (Phil 2:6–11) while keeping in mind the introductory words in verse 5: "Make your own the mind of Christ Jesus." This is what Christian life means (see Eph 5:1–2: imitate God . . . follow the way of love, that is, live in love, in the same way as Christ who loved us).

This whole process begins with our baptism (Rom 6:1–11), and the rest of our Christian life consists of participating at each moment, each day, in the mystery of Christ's death and Resurrection. "I am resurrected *with* Christ." I must convince myself of that reality. I must place that reality at the heart of my being, at the core of my work, at the center of my relations with all those with whom I come in contact. It must color my vision of the world. What a change in my thinking this way of looking at things will make! What dynamic energy it will give to my life, to how I see myself and others, to what I do, to how I view the world!

It is here that we find "the glorious freedom as children of God". He liberates us, and with us he liberates all of creation (Rom 8:12–24).

In ending this contemplation *I will converse intimately*

— with the risen Jesus . . . reliving with him the marvelous scenes of his apparitions
— with our Lady, asking her for her faith
— with one or another of the apostles: Peter . . . John . . .

I will conclude with an Our Father.

THIRTIETH DAY

THE FORTY DAYS BETWEEN
EASTER AND THE ASCENSION

Put yourself in the presence of God and make the prayer beginning the exercise.
Ask him to inspire you.

I will call to mind the *history of the events.* During a period of forty days the resurrected Jesus appeared to his friends. According to the accounts of Paul and Luke it would seem that these apparitions were numerous.

We can classify these apparitions into two categories:

1. There are the apparitions of "identification and recognition of the resurrected Christ". These were either to a particular apostle or to individuals who were not apostles. Jesus wanted to establish the fact that he was indeed the same Jesus of Nazareth whom they had known, even though he was now living in a way that was different from before.

2. There are the apparitions made to a group of apostles. In these Jesus emphasized the new mission he was giving his apostles. These apparitions embody the different steps the resurrected Jesus took in founding the Church.

Composition of Place

No one place; kaleidoscopic, scattered scenes. Perhaps it would be best to live with a group of apostles and to pick up all the news in these wonder-filled days.

193

I will ask for *what I want and desire.* Here it will be the grace to be glad and to rejoice intensely because of the great glory and joy of Christ our Lord.

First Point: The Apparitions during the Forty Days

The retreatant may choose, as he desires, one or another of the scenes found at the end of each of the four Gospel accounts where the appearances of the risen Christ can be found. Or he might be drawn to rereading verses 3 to 9 in chapter 15 of St. Paul's First Letter to the Corinthians. What we are going to do here is take the beginning of Acts (1:1–14) and the last part of Luke (24:1–53).

1. "In the time after his suffering he showed them in many convincing ways that he was alive, appearing to them over the course of forty days and speaking to them about the Kingdom of God" (Acts 1:3).

He did so to persuade them of the fact that he was truly resurrected. This is what he did with the disciples on the way to Emmaus when he performed a particular action. They recognized the risen Jesus in the breaking of the bread. And to the Eleven he said, "Touch me, and see that a ghost does not have flesh and bones as I do" (Luke 24:39). "They gave him a piece of cooked fish, which he took and ate in their presence" (Luke 24:42–43). He invites the unbelieving Thomas to "take your finger and examine my hands. Put your hand into my side" (John 20:26–28). "Finally, as they were at table, Jesus was revealed to the Eleven" (Mark 16:14), and then the evangelist continues, "He reproached them for their incredulity and obstinacy because they had refused to believe those who had seen him after he had risen." After these apparitions they believed. "My Lord and my God", said Thomas. Peter, in the discourse he would later give at Cornelius' house, would say, "They killed him, finally, hanging him on a tree, only to have God raise him up on the third day and grant that he be seen, not by all, but only by such witnesses as had been chosen beforehand by God—by us who ate and drank with him after he rose from the dead" (Acts 10:41).

He did so in order that they would come to understand that all was accomplished "according to the Scriptures". Consider this beautiful text from Luke (24:44–49): "Then he opened their minds to the understanding of the Scriptures. And he said to them, 'Thus it is written that the Messiah must suffer and rise from the dead on the third day. . . . You are witnesses of this.' " Reflect as well on what he told the disciples on their way to Emmaus (Luke 24:25–27).

And finally he did so in order to give them his joy. The words of the resurrected Lord were: "*Pax vobis.* Peace be with you." He played his part as "consoler", "comforter", before sending "the Holy Spirit, the Consoler".

2. "He spoke to them about the Kingdom of God" (Acts 1:3).

They certainly had need for such words. Recall the "distress" and the "disappointment" of the disciples on their way to Emmaus and the chagrin of all his followers after the Passion. "*Sperabamus:* We were hoping." Which is to imply that "we will no longer hope!" (Luke 24:21).

And the Kingdom they were hoping for was still the kingdom of a reconstructed Israel! Jesus told them in a number of ways that his Kingdom was, on the contrary, a Kingdom of salvation: "Go, baptize . . . teach". They were to preach "in his name, penance for the forgiveness of sins . . . to all the nations beginning at Jerusalem" (Luke 24:47).

3. And he ordered them: "Stay in the city, then, until you are clothed with power from on high" (Luke 24:49).

Second Point: The Ascension (Acts 1:6–11)

On the Mount of Olives, "a mere sabbath's journey away" from Jerusalem, facing the city and facing Calvary, up above Gethsemane.

The eyes look down on Palestine. The heart goes beyond the horizons of the whole world and of all times. This is the place, the site for the ceremonious scene where the risen Jesus would bid his earthly farewell.

This is the hour for Jesus, the Word made flesh, to enter in a perceptible way into the glory of his Father . . . *ceremoniously* . . . historically before witnesses, we might say. The scene has its meaning *in relation to us*. Because the resurrected Jesus is already *"apud Patrem,* in the Father's presence".

The scene unfolds according to these thematic developments:

Jesus and his disciples, "having met together", were now assembled.

They were still questioning him: "Lord, are you going to restore the rule to Israel now?" (They had not made much progress as far as that topic was concerned.)

Jesus answered them, "You will receive power when the Holy Spirit comes down on you; then you are to be my witnesses in Jerusalem, throughout Judea and Samaria, yes, even to the ends of the earth" (Acts 1:8; see also Mark 16:15–20; Matt 28:16–20).

Jesus "was taken up to heaven" before his apostles, who "fell down to do him reverence" (Luke 24:51–52).

Two angels proclaimed Christ's return (Acts 1:11).

The "christic" cycle is thus accomplished. The liturgy of the Mass recalls the mystery of the ascension on two occasions in the canon, both in relation to the death and the Resurrection of Christ. It is as if the ascension were the Father's perceptible acceptance of the whole redemption of Christ.

In the Epistle to the Ephesians St. Paul speaks of the ascension in chapter 4, beginning with verse 7. He presents it as the inauguration of the body of Christ and the beginning of "that perfect man who is Christ come to full stature". The scene of the ascension manifests the "recapitulating" role of the risen Christ: "The Head of the body"; "the Head of everything in the heavens and everything on earth" (Col 1; Eph 1; 2; 3).

Third Point: The Return to the Cenacle

The hearts of the apostles are already filled with hope for the coming of the Holy Spirit, promised by Jesus. What a difference here from the night of Good Friday! Even though Jesus had left them when he ascended to the Father, "They returned to Jerusalem filled with joy" (Luke 24:52). Savor this difference and contrast it with the attitude of the apostles on Good Friday night.

"So from the Mount of Olives . . . they went back to Jerusalem . . . and when they reached the city they went to the upper room where they *were staying*" (Acts then lists the eleven apostles by name: 1:13). The narrative then continues: "Together they devoted themselves to constant prayer. There were some women in their company, and Mary the Mother of Jesus, and his brothers."

Luke adds a nice touch to his account: "There [in Jerusalem] they were to be found in the temple constantly, speaking the praises of God" (Luke 24:53).

It was then, at the initiative of Peter, that the Eleven and "the brothers—there were about 120 people in the congregation"—proceeded to replace Judas. What Peter will say about this should be kept in mind: "Out of the men who have been with us the whole time that the Lord Jesus was living with us, from the time when John was baptizing until the day when he was taken up from us—one must be appointed to serve with us as a witness to his Resurrection" (Acts 1:21-22). With these words he was defining clearly the identity, the role and the mission of the man who was to become part of the College of the Eleven. Then, "as the lot fell to Matthias, he was listed as one of the twelve apostles".
I shall talk over these matters in a conversation

— with the risen Jesus: "My Lord and my God!" I will hear at the center of my being his *"Pax vobis"*.

— with Mary, the Mother and focal point of the group awaiting the coming of Pentecost.

— with Peter, head of the young Church, before whom Mary acquiesced.

I shall love to repeat, to savor, one or another of the words uttered by one of the fortunate individuals who shared in an apparition of the risen Jesus. I shall choose one of these words that speaks most to my heart, such as "Rabbouni" (Magdalen), "my Lord and my God" (Thomas), etc.

I will end by saying the Our Father.

THIRTY-FIRST DAY

PENTECOST AND THE CHURCH

St. Ignatius does not include a contemplation on the subject of Pentecost in the *Spiritual Exercises,* but what he does offer us is a long list of "rules that should be observed to foster the true attitude of mind we ought to have in the Church militant". It has seemed to me that in order to give these rules their broadest sense, it would be helpful to put them into the context of a Gospel contemplation on the mystery of Pentecost. From this list of his eighteen rules we cite here the three principal ones:

1. "Leaving aside every judgment of our own, we ought to keep our minds inclined to obeying promptly in all things the true Spouse of Christ our Lord, our holy Mother the hierarchical Church."

2. "To deal rightly in all matters, I must be ever ready to believe that what I see before me as white is black, if the hierarchical Church clearly teaches it as such. We must be really convinced that between Christ our Lord, who is the Bridegroom, and the Church, his Bride, there is the same Spirit, which governs us and directs us for the good of our souls. The reason is that it is the same Spirit and Lord who has given us the Ten Commandments who governs and directs our holy Mother the Church."

3. "If it is true we must esteem above all the zealous service of God our Lord through love, then we should also praise with great conviction the fear of his Divine Majesty. Not only is filial fear a good and a very holy thing, but, when it is not present, servile fear is a powerful help to keep us from mortal sin; and once one extricates himself from such sin, he very easily advances in filial

199

fear, which is wholly agreeable to God our Lord because it is not attained except by divine love."

Place yourself in God's presence and make the prayer beginning the contemplation.
  Ask him to inspire you.

I will recall the *history of this mystery* as it is presented in Acts 2:104.

Composition of Place

The Cenacle, that is, "the upstairs room where they [the twelve apostles and Mary] were staying".
  I will ask for *what I want and desire.* Here it will be to have the true sense of the Church and to experience great joy and happiness for having been called to be one of her members through faith and baptism, through penance and the Eucharist.

First Point: Pentecost

  1. Before the actual event takes place:

  At the place where they were accustomed to meet, the apostles gathered together with Mary to pray.

  2. The event itself:

  Here is what we learn from the account in the Acts of the Apostles: "When the day of Pentecost came it found them gathered in one place. Suddenly from up in the sky there came a noise like a strong, driving wind that was heard all through the house where they were seated. Tongues as of fire appeared, which parted and came to rest on each of them. All were filled with the Holy Spirit. They began to express themselves in foreign tongues and make bold proclamations as the Spirit prompted them."

3. After the event:

The gift of tongues: indeed, this was needed because the apostles would go to preach the Gospel "to the ends of the earth": "Go, teach . . . "

Transformation of the apostles: "There were a few who remarked with a sneer, 'They have had too much new wine!' And Peter responded, 'You must realize that these men are not drunk, as you seem to think. It is only nine in the morning! No.'" But they are drunk with the rapture of the Spirit.

And thus was born the first of the Christian "communities". These communities were so admirable (Acts 2:42–47; 4:32–35), in spite of the inevitable "miseries"—wonderful because of prayer, poverty, sharing of goods, simplicity. The dynamism of these young Christians! Such is always the case whenever the Church is "planted".

Second Point: Who Is the Holy Spirit?

1. According to the Bible he is the Principle of all life (see Gen 1:2; 2:7; Ezek 37, particularly verses 5, 9, 14):

He is the one who makes his presence known at the Annunciation and at the baptism of our Lord. St. Paul attributes Christ's Resurrection and our own to him (Rom 8:9–11).

It is because of these activities that the Holy Spirit is described in the Bible as fire, living water, storm, light, blood . . . effusion, expansion, union: "When you send forth your spirit, they are created, and you renew the face of the earth" (Ps 104:30).

2. He is the Spirit of love that unites the Father and Son in the Trinity:

He proceeds from the Father and is the Spirit of the Son. He is the Spirit, the great Principle of unity between the Father and Son and between the Son and ourselves (see Jesus' last discourse: John 14:1 to 17:26).

Through him "we participate in divine nature". See St. Paul's first letter to the Thessalonians (5:23): "May the God of peace make you perfect in holiness. May he preserve you whole and entire, *spirit,* soul, and body, irreproachable at the coming of our Lord Jesus Christ"; or St. Augustine: "Man is composed of a body, a soul . . . and the Holy Spirit."

The Holy Spirit dwells through this mysterious *habitation* in me:

— Spirit of life: Through him, I am a branch of Christ the vine.

— Spirit of truth: doctrinal and mystical.

— Spirit of strength and courage: "The Lord is the Spirit, and where the Spirit of the Lord is, there is freedom" (2 Cor 3:17).

— Spirit of joy.

— Spirit of piety and faith: "No one can say, 'Jesus is Lord,' except in the Holy Spirit" (1 Cor 12:3). It is the Spirit who "prays in me" (Rom 8:14–17, 26–27; Gal 4:6).

— Spirit of unity and charity; the fruits of the Spirit according to St. Paul (Gal 5:22).

— See the seven gifts of the Holy Spirit according to Isaiah (11:2).

— In the framework of this meditation reread St. Paul's magnificent Hymn of Charity (1 Cor 13:1 to 14:40).

— He is Love.

— He is the divine reality of Love.

— He is the gift of Love.

— He is the genuineness of Love.

— He is the productivity of Love.

"*Deus caritas:* God is Love."

Third Point: The Holy Spirit Is All of This for Me Only because He Is the Soul of the Mystical Body, Which Is the Church

The Church is Jesus Christ continued on to this very day for me. The Church is:

— my principle of life. It is through her, in her, that I have been baptized, pardoned, fed with the Eucharist, sanctified.

— the place of my prayer. She organizes my liturgical prayer and safeguards my mystical prayer. The Mass is the center of my prayer, the memorial of the "mystery of Christ".

— the principle of unity and charity with my brothers and sisters, baptized and nonbaptized alike.

— the vitalizing and directing principle of what I do, of my apostolate as someone who has been baptized, confirmed, and, if I am an ordained priest, of my priestly functions (see 1 Cor 13).

In return, the most personal gifts that the Holy Spirit gives me are for the Church, and I received them in the Church (see Eph 4:11–13; 1 Pet 4:10–11).

We can apply a most beautiful Psalm, Psalm 87, to the Church:

> *Of Philistia, Tyre, Ethiopia,*
> *"Here so and so was born", men say.*
> *But all call Zion "Mother",*
> *since all were born in her.*
> *It is he who makes her what she is,*
> *he, the Most High, Yahweh . . .*
> *And there will be princes dancing there.*
> *All find their home in you.*

Pentecost—it is realized every day . . . *Veni Creator Spiritus.* Here the plan of God is at last realized, the veritable "foundation", the movement in which I must insert myself. The movement that is historical and at the same time eternal, personal and communitarian, temporal and eschatological.

I will talk over these things in conversation with the Holy Spirit. Ever since the day I was baptized, he has made his dwelling in my soul, along with the Father and the Son. He is, in the words of St. Francis de Sales, "the heart of my heart". I shall say over slowly the hymn of Pentecost: *"Veni, sancte Spiritus",* with Christ, "the Head of the Mystical Body", with the Virgin Mary of the Cenacle.

I will end with the Our Father.

THIRTY-SECOND DAY

CONTEMPLATION TO ATTAIN AND LIVE IN THE LOVE OF GOD

This contemplation summarizes, as it were, the whole of the Spiritual Exercises. It provides the retreatant, who will shortly be going back to his regular schedule, with a basically spiritual way of looking at things, a vision of the world, a solid, simple spirituality that he can implement each day at his work or in dealing with the problems of life he has to face. The permanent setting of the "celestial court" where St. Ignatius now situates the retreatant; the simple yet demanding law of "love for love" that now supersedes the "praise, reverence, and serve God our Lord" of the Foundation; the most humble and filial concept of "abandonment", which now takes the place of difficult concepts contained in the Exercises, like indifference and election; all this realism of faith and nature, this fusion of spirit and action in the same movement of life—all of these features make the Contemplation to Attain Love of God the synthesis of Christian life. It is the Foundation all over again, if one wishes to put it that way, but now it is the Foundation lived out in every phase of one's life, from the most commonplace to the most adventuresome. Christian life is a relationship of permanent love between the Father, who is in heaven, and his Son, who lives on earth in men and in creation. "In him we live and move and have our being . . . for we too are his offspring" (Acts 17:28).

PRELIMINARY NOTE

St. Ignatius recommended that before beginning this exercise, it would be good to call attention to these two points:

1. Love ought to manifest itself in deeds rather than in words.

2. Love consists in a mutual sharing of goods. The person who loves communicates to his beloved all or part of what he has, and likewise the beloved with the lover. Hence, if one has knowledge, he shares it with the one who does not have it; the same goes for honors or riches. And thus there are always a mutual giving and receiving.

Such are the fundamental laws of love or of true friendship.

Place yourself *in the presence of God and the whole celestial court,* the angels and saints, just as in the Preface of the Mass when we are invited to do so by "joining with the choirs of heaven to sing, Holy, Holy, Holy."

And this is not a simple *composition of place;* this is a permanent reality.

Make the prayer beginning the contemplation and ask God to inspire you.

I will ask for *what I want and desire.* Here this will be an intimate knowledge of the many and wonderful gifts I have received from God, so that in return, filled with gratitude, I may love and serve his Divine Majesty in all things.

"Lord, give me new eyes, a new heart, so that henceforth I shall be able to see the heavens and earth as the new heavens and the new earth, as was promised by your Word to those in whom your Spirit of love would dwell."

First Point: Love Is a Gift, a Continuous Mutual Exchange of All That One Has and Is

God has given to me all that I possess: the gift of creation, redemption, and my particular personal gifts.

With much love I shall take into account how much our Lord has done for me, how much he has given me of *what he has:* "O Divine Goodness".

Through his grace, he has even given me *what he is.* According to his divine plan, he gives himself to me as much as he possibly can.

I will reflect now for a moment on myself. According to all reason and justice, I for my part ought to offer his Divine Majesty all the good things that I have and myself along with them. And this I ought to do as one moved by an outburst of great love. For this reason I ought to say to him:

> *Take, Lord, and receive*
> *all my liberty,*
> *my memory, my understanding, and my entire will,*
> *all that I have and possess.*
> *You have given all to me.*
> *To you, Lord, I return it.*
> *All is yours:*
> *Dispose of it wholly according to your will.*
> *Give me your love and your grace;*
> *this is sufficient for me.*

Second Point: Love Is a Reciprocal Being Present to the Other at Each Moment

I will look at how God dwells in his creatures, in material beings, giving them existence; in plants, giving them life; in animals, giving them sensation; in men, giving them understanding through their intellect.

So he dwells in me, giving me existence, life, sensation, intelligence.

More than this, he has made me his temple, first of all by creating me "in his image and likeness" but especially by dwelling within me through the grace of my baptism.

Then I will reflect on myself. According to all reason and justice I ought on my part to endeavor to live in God ("to live in":

an expression dear to the Apostle St. John), to make my dwelling place in him, to make him present to me at every moment and me present to him, so that I belong to him completely. And I will then renew my offering as one who would make an offering moved by an outburst of great love: *"Take, Lord, and receive."*

Third Point: Love Is a Total Sharing in Every Activity

I will consider how God works and labors for me and for all creatures on the face of the earth. He conducts himself as one who prepares and disposes everything for the one he loves.

More than this, he works and labors in me by giving me everything that I have so that I myself can work and labor—and especially he works in me through his grace, giving my work an *infinite* effectiveness. The result is that in some way my life is divinized.

I will then reflect on myself. According to all reason and justice, I for my part ought to work and labor for God, giving myself entirely to his service and his glory and showing his Divine Majesty all the good and helpful things I do in the place here on earth where his Providence has placed me. And I will renew my offering as one would do moved by an outburst of great love: *"Take, Lord, and receive . . . "*

Fourth Point: In Love We Belong to Each Other, We Partake of What Is Ours

Just as all rays shine forth from the sun, as waters gush from the spring, so do all that is good and every gift I have come from God: my limited power from his infinite and sovereign power, my limited goodness from his goodness; my piety from his holiness, my compassion from his compassion, etc.

Especially, the grace in me comes to me as a gratuitous gift from his divine life.

I shall reflect on myself. According to all reason and justice, I for my part ought to attach myself to the Source and open myself completely to Divine Influence so that there is nothing that encumbers or dilutes his radiant activity in me. And I shall repeat once again my offering, as someone who makes an offering moved by an outburst of great love: *"Take, Lord, and receive . . . "*

What a transformation this makes of my whole life here below! I can at last realize this wonderful ideal that God from the very beginning proposed to man: "Hear, O Israel! The Lord is our God, the Lord alone! Therefore, you shall love the Lord, your God, with all your heart, and with all your soul, and with all your strength. Take to heart these words that I enjoin on you today. Drill them into your children. Speak of them at home and abroad, whether you are busy or at rest. Bind them onto your wrist as a sign and let them be as a pendant on your forehead. Write them on your houses and on your gates" (Deut 6:4-9). Better yet: I can say to God: Abba! Father; because I am his true son in Jesus Christ. I am, I ought in truth to be, "the image and likeness" of God, who is Love.

I shall talk these things over in a colloquy:

With the Father "from whom every family in heaven and on earth takes its name" (Eph 3:15). I shall recall these words from the Epistle to the Romans (12:1): "And now, brothers, I beg you through the mercy of God to offer your bodies as a living sacrifice holy and acceptable to God, your spiritual worship." I shall humbly ask him for this "love of Christ that surpasses all knowledge", so that I "may attain to the fullness of God himself" (Eph 3:19).

With Christ our Lord. I shall speak to his heart. Once again I will tell him, "You have loved me, and you have delivered yourself for me." What should I do for Christ in return?

With our Lady, our "Mother of Divine Love".

And I shall complete this contemplation with the Our Father. In order to say it well, I shall lose myself in this overwhelming current of love within the Trinity, which goes between the Father, Son, and Holy Spirit and then diffuses itself within the heart of every man and finally returns to the Father through Jesus Christ, now resurrected and exalted. Indeed: Our Father!

The Prayer That Includes All Things Within Itself and That Says Everything There Is to Be Said: "Our Father . . ."

The Fathers of the Church and the greatest authors of mystical prayer have taken great pleasure in commenting on the Our Father. We should now better understand why.

There is a Carmelite monastery built near the top of the Mount of Olives. The walls of its cloisters are covered with marble plaques on which the words of the *Pater Noster* are engraved in each of the world's principal languages. Now that we have contemplated God's love, does not such a display seem normal and reasonable?

And so it is that the very peak of our souls, in the very center of all that we think and do, the Lord's Prayer ought to be inscribed in living letters:

Our Father
Who art in heaven,
Hallowed by thy name.
Thy Kingdom come;
Thy will be done
On earth as it is in heaven.
Give us this day our daily bread,
And forgive us our trespasses,
As we forgive those who trespass against us;
And lead us not into temptation,
But deliver us from evil.

If this retreat has helped us simply to recite the Our Father with more faith in our understanding and more love in our heart, its purpose has been achieved. We are more the "sons of God".

TO CHRIST OUR LORD

Soul of Christ, be my sanctification;
Body of Christ, be my salvation;
Blood of Christ's side, fill all my veins;
Water of Christ's side, wash out my stains;
Passion of Christ, my comfort be;
O good Jesus, listen to me.
In thy wounds I hide me,
Never let me be parted from thy side.
Guard me should the foe assail me,
Call me when my life shall fail me.
Bid me to come to thee above
With thy saints to sing thy love,
World without end.
Amen.[1]

TO OUR LADY

Hail, Mary, full of grace!
The Lord is with thee;
Blessed art thou among women,
And blessed is the fruit of thy womb, Jesus.
Holy Mary, Mother of God,
Pray for us sinners,
Now and at the hour of our death.
Amen.

---

[1] This prayer, whose origin was probably Franciscan, goes back at least to the beginning of the fourteenth century, perhaps to the time of John XXII. It was very popular during the lifetime of St. Ignatius.

COME O SANCTIFYING SPIRIT!

(Veni Sancte Spiritus)

Come, O Spirit of sanctity, from the glory of heaven
and send forth the radiance of your light.
Father of all the poor, light and peace of all hearts,
come with your countless gifts!
Consoler in desolation; refreshment full of loveliness;
come, dear friend of my soul!
In weariness send repose;
breathe gently the cool refreshing breeze;
console the desolate who weep alone.
O Light of beatitude, make our hearts ready;
come, enter into our souls.
Without your grace, man stands alone;
he cannot be good or sure.
Cleanse what is soiled; heal what is wounded;
moisten what is arid.
Bend the stubborn will; warm the cold heart;
guide the wandering footstep!
Holy Spirit, we beg you to give us grace
through your sevenfold power.
Give us merit for the present,
and one day beatitude when we have finished our earthly sojourn.
Amen. Alleluia!

TO THE HOLY TRINITY

Glory be to the Father,
And to the Son,
And to the Holy Spirit;
As it was in the beginning, is now, and ever shall be,
world without end.
Amen.

A Sentence Composed by St. Ignatius
That Summarizes the Spiritual Exercises

"Sic Deo fide quasi rerum successum omnis a te,
nihil a Deo penderet. Ita tamen iis omnem operam
admove quasi tu nihil Deus solus omnia sit facturus."

Here is a translation of this admirable formula for Christian life
and action:

"Trust in God as though the entire success of your
affairs depended on you and not at all on God, and at the same
time give yourself completely to work as if you were not able to
do anything yourself and God alone could do everything."[2]

---

[2] For a commentary on this text, see Gaston Fessard, *La dialectique des Exercises Spirituels* (Paris: Aubier, Editions Montaigne, 1957), 305–63.

Instructions for the One Who Directs a Retreatant

1. Be sparing in your counsels and in the explanation you give on the subject for meditation or contemplation. If relevant, point out the place where the Scriptural text dealing with the subject can be found and faithfully relate the facts contained in the meditation or contemplation. Present your explanation in a summary manner.

2. If, during the course of the retreat, the retreatant does not experience any spiritual movement, that is, if he does not feel inflamed with love or does not experience darkness of soul or turmoil of spirit, ask him if he is faithful in making the exercises at the appointed times and if he is honestly following the directions that were given to him. Do not hesitate to ask him to go into detail in these matters. At the same time, remember that a person can certainly make a very good retreat in that "state of tranquility" we spoke of when dealing with the election, that is, when the soul is conscious of going through the Spiritual Exercises with much interior freedom and peace.

3. If you see that the retreatant is in desolation or is tempted, do not deal either harshly or severely with him but be kindly and good. Encourage and strengthen him for the future. If you see clearly what is taking place in him, and if you think this knowledge can help him, tell him about it. Help him to make ready for the consolation that undoubtedly will come after the storm passes.

4. Should the retreatant be given the rules that enable him to discern, with the light of the Holy Spirit, the different spiritual movements taking place in his soul? The decision should be made according to the need of each retreatant. Such a presentation is indispensable in certain cases, but in others—when dealing, for example, with persons who overscrutinize everything or who are scrupulous—this information could be harmful.

5. Discretion and prudence are particularly needed during the course of the First Week, when one is dealing with a retreatant who is unskilled in spiritual matters and who is still meeting head on with such worldly obstacles as human respect, an excessive fear of suffering or failure, and the like. The rules of the First Week could perhaps prove useful for him, but the rules of the Second Week will be harmful. The subject matter of these rules of the Second Week is too subtle and advanced for him to draw profit from them.

6. When you see that the retreatant is being tempted to something evil under the appearance of a good, then, if it seems helpful and expedient, this is the right time to talk with him about the matter contained in the rules of the Second Week. Normally the soul that is progressing along the illuminative way (which corresponds to the exercises of the Second Week) is more often tempted under the appearance of the good. This type of temptation is more rare during the course of the purgative way, which corresponds to the exercises of the First Week.

7. During the times when the retreatant is inflamed with love for spiritual things, warn him against making any commitment or taking any ill-considered, hasty vow—all the more reason to do so if you know the person has a susceptible and flighty temperament. Even though *in itself* a good work done under a vow is more meritorious than one preformed without a vow, and even though one can always encourage a person to enter the religious life in which he knows that the vows of obedience, poverty, and chastity are taken, nevertheless, a director always has to take under the most serious consideration the particular temperament and gifts of the retreatant. Would these vows and these promises be a help or a constraint for this particular individual? Would such vows and promises be a fountain of peace or a source of troubles for *this* person here and now? This is the question that should ultimately determine our attitude in such a case.

8. During the retreat, do not influence the retreatant to opt for

evangelical poverty or for one state of life as opposed to another or for any other kind of commitment. It is true that outside of the Exercises it may be permissible and even praiseworthy to encourage all who give evidence of being able to choose celibacy, virginity, the religious life, and every form of religious perfection. However, during the course of the Spiritual Exercises, it is wiser and better for the director to motivate the retreatant to seek only the divine will so that our Creator and Lord will communicate himself to the soul, embrace it with love and praise of himself, and dispose it for the way where it could better serve him in the future. For this reason do not encourage the person toward one side or the other but remain at equilibrium between the two. Let the Creator deal with the creature *without any intermediary* and the creature with the Creator in the same way. Such a frame of mind respects more God's initiative and the soul's freedom.

9. Adapt the Exercises to the wishes of the persons who want to make them, taking into account their dispositions, that is, their age, education, and spiritual experience. Never propose anything that goes beyond the soul's resources. At the same time, give to each person, according to the spiritual dispositions that he brings to the retreat, whatever will be helpful to him in the future. For this reason, offer to the person who aspires to lead an ordinary Christian life the Particular Examination (p. 49) and then the General Examination (p. 48), along with a method to enable him to meditate for half an hour each morning on the Commandments, the capital sins, etc. (pp. 43–44). Also recommend that he go to confession weekly and that, if possible, he receive Communion every fifteen or eight days and even, if he desires it, every day. Encourage him to take on some of the spiritual works of mercy, to apply himself on behalf of the poor, of those who suffer and are distressed, and the like. Encourage him to live sincerely the simple life of the baptized, to follow the liturgical life of the Church with fervor, and especially to make the Bible (particularly the Gospels) his constant companion, his "book of life".

Similarly, if you see that the person making the retreat does not have the natural or spiritual abilities that will enable him to draw profit from the Exercises, he should not become involved in any matter dealing with the election of a way of life or in any other exercises that go beyond those of the First Week. This is especially the case when there are other retreatants capable of greater progress and the time is limited for you to deal with everyone.

10. You can have the person who is busy with public affairs or is involved with other important works, but who nevertheless does have the desired aptitudes to profit from a retreat, and who would be able to put aside an hour and a half each day doing the Exercises—you can have such a person make the different exercises, and you should adapt them the best way you can to his particular situation.

IT IS EXTREMELY IMPORTANT THAT DURING
THE COURSE OF THE SPIRITUAL EXERCISES
THE RETREATANT FEEL WITHIN HIMSELF
"THE FREEDOM OF THE SONS OF GOD"
SO THAT IT IS ONLY THE HOLY SPIRIT
WHO INSPIRES HIS DECISIONS.

AFTER THE RETREAT
HE MUST BE CONSCIENTIOUSLY RESPONSIBLE,
AS A SON OF GOD,
IN IMPLEMENTING WHAT GOD'S WILL IS
FOR HIM.

How God Makes Known His Will
to Each One of Us at Every Minute of the Day

Love between two spiritual beings demands a union of wills.[1] The relation of love between God and man implies that at every moment and in every circumstance man seeks what God wants him to do, and he does it.

How can man know what God's will for him is? First of all, through the Ten Commandments, the evangelical counsels, and the general directives found in Scripture. In addition, through such events in our lives that God wills, permits, or tolerates. This Providence of God watches over all people, and so it pertains to everyone in general.

But there is something more for each one of us, a particular will of God covering each moment of our existence. How can I know it? It makes itself known to me at the very center of my being by an imperious yet whispering call inviting me to choose this line of action in preference to all others. Undoubtedly this call is the natural reaction of my conscience as a person before a situation in which I find myself involved, but because I am a Christian the call is also the reaction of a conscience enlightened and strengthened by grace. The voice of the Lord, so to speak, is within me by virtue of two different conditions. It is there first of all as the judgment of a human conscience, and at the same time it is there as the motion of baptismal grace. This call is usually referred to by spiritual writers as the "inspiration of the Holy Spirit".

---

[1] This statement refers to the human soul insofar as it understands, desires, and pursues the purpose of its existence; it is the depth of one's being that gives meaning to what constitutes his personality and way of acting.

The place of such inspirations of the Holy Spirit in the life of a Christian is therefore considerable. It is through inspirations that God informs me at each moment what his will is for me here and now. For the Christian the dramatic debate between good and evil, which takes place at the center of every conscience, consists of consenting to or resisting the inspirations of the Holy Spirit.

Let us hear what St. Francis de Sales, an expert in this field, has to say about this subject: "After God had formed man from the clay of the ground, . . . he breathed into his nostrils the breath of life and made of man a living person [Gen 2:7]—in other words, a soul that gave life, movement, and activity to Adam's body. The same eternal God breathes, infuses into our souls the inspirations of the spiritual life, so that, in the words of St. Paul, they become living souls [1 Cor 15:45]—in other words, souls that give life, movement, feeling, and activity to the operations of grace."[2] In this manner inspiration is as necessary to the life of our soul as breathing is to the life of our body. How does it function? "By inspiration", again writes St. Francis de Sales, "we mean all those interior attractions, movements of the heart, pangs of conscience, and illuminations of the mind by which God, in his fatherly love and care, predisposes our hearts with his blessings, to awaken, stir, urge, and attract us to virtue, charity and good resolutions, in fact to everything that serves our eternal good."[3] Inspirations therefore play a major role in the continuous struggle between good and evil that goes on in a person's conscience. They form an integral part of our spiritual life.

It would seem that for a generous soul the way leading toward the good should be clear and simple, that it would be enough for him to follow the motions of the Holy Spirit. The fact is, however, that the process is far more difficult than it would appear at first sight. The soul itself is subject to illusions, and Satan, in order to carry out his intrigue, can at times transform himself into an angel of light. Given this fact, the following bit of advice from St.

[2] St. Francis de Sales, *The Love of God*, 340.
[3] St. Francis de Sales, *Introduction to the Devout Life*, 76.

Francis de Sales is extremely valuable: "Before you consent to inspirations concerning important or extraordinary matters," he writes, "seek the advice of your confessor, that he may examine whether they are true or false and so preserve you from deception; for the devil often sends false inspirations to deceive those who receive them readily, but he can never deceive those who humbly obey their confessor."[4] Elsewhere he repeats a few words full of wise advice, which he has already given in the eighth book of *The Love of God,* on how to recognize "legitimate inspirations": "It comes therefore to this: the three finest, surest proofs of the genuine character of inspiration are perseverance in contrast to fickleness, peace of soul in contrast to impulsive anxiety, humble obedience in contrast to stubborn willfulness."[5]

We can better appreciate the rules St. Ignatius gives for understanding, analyzing, and appreciating the different movements that can take place in the soul of the person making the retreat when we see them within the general framework of the role inspirations play in our spiritual life.

---

[4] St. Francis de Sales, *Introduction to the Devout Life,* 78.
[5] St. Francis de Sales, *The Love of God,* 351.

RULES

For Understanding, as Far as Possible, the Different Movements Produced in the Soul and for Recognizing Those That Are Good and Accepting Them and Those That Are Bad and Rejecting Them

FOREWORD[1]

We should introduce here the well-known term *Discernment of Spirits* and make a brief commentary on it. It is a term that immerses us in the most ancient tradition of spiritual literature. From the first days of his conversion, St. Ignatius experienced different "spirits". Speaking about his convalescence at Loyola, he mentioned in his autobiographical account that "step by step he came to recognize the difference between the two spirits that moved him, the one being from the evil spirit, the other from God".[2] It would seem that Ignatius' personal experience ought to be enough to tell us what is meant by the *discernment of spirits*. But as a matter of fact, the problem is not simple because the word *spirit* is itself complex. It means the state of one's soul or the driving force of one's conscience toward good or evil. But what is the origin of this state or of these motions? They could arise from one's personality, and we are readily aware of the insights that

---

[1] This first set of rules is more suited to the First Week of the Exercises, that is, during the time of the retreatant's first conversion; but they are also quite useful for the one making the Exercises during the three remaining weeks or even when, after the retreat is over, he goes back to his ordinary occupations.

[2] St. Ignatius of Loyola, *St. Ignatius' Own Story as Told to Luis Gonzalez de Camara,* trans. William J. Young, S.J. (Chicago: Loyola University Press, 1980), 10.

modern psychology, when prudently used, can give us in this area. They can also come from outside forces such as the weather, one's state of health, different events taking place in one's life, and so forth. Lastly, as St. Ignatius states in the text we have cited, they can come from God or Satan, from the angels of God or from the demons. Whatever its origin, this state of soul creates a problem for the conscience the moment it inclines the person to choose this good or that evil. St. Ignatius realized the problem. In the first rule for discerning the movements within the soul, he says, speaking of the good spirit: "Making use of the light of reason, he will sting their conscience with remorse and disturb it." For our purposes here, it is enough to assert that the rules we are going to list below have their value at the level of the human conscience, enlightened by faith and aided by the grace of fortitude. Discernment of spirits consists of understanding and recognizing those movements that take place in a person's conscience *as a result of the action of the Holy Spirit.* Hence, we can now see how discriminating the theory of St. Francis de Sales described above is and how prudent the counsels he recommended are.

First Rule. In the case of those who go from one capital sin to another, Satan is accustomed to propose apparent pleasures. He has them imagining pleasures and sensual delights so as to hold them and plunge them even deeper in their vices and sins.

The good spirit acts on them in the opposite way. Making use of the *natural* law of reason, he will sting their conscience with remorse and disturb it.

Second Rule. In the case of those who are earnestly making an effort to free themselves from faults and are endeavoring to go from good to better in the service of God our Savior, the method pursued is the opposite of that mentioned in the first rule. Here the plan of the evil spirit consists in harassing the person, in making him sad, in putting obstacles in his way. He causes the soul to become upset through false reasoning, which he sets up to prevent it from making progress. The plan of the good spirit consists in giving the person courage and strength, consolations, tears, inspirations, and peace. He minimizes the difficulties, and he removes obstacles so that the soul makes progress in doing good.

Third Rule: Spiritual consolation. I call consolation the interior movement when the soul begins to become so inflamed with love for its Creator and Lord that it can no longer love any created thing on the face of the earth in itself but only in the Creator of all things.

Spiritual consolation is also when the soul sheds tears that flow from the love it has for its Lord, whether this is from sorrow for sin or from the memory of the Passion of Christ our Lord, or from any other consideration immediately directed to his service and praise (see discussion of tears on p. 55).

Finally, I call consolation every increase of faith, hope, and charity and all interior joy that invites and draws the soul toward the things of heaven and spiritual good by filling it with rest and peace in the presence of its Creator and Lord. (This definition is of capital importance for correct understanding of the fundamentals of Ignatian spirituality and even of all Christian spirituality. All things are to be judged and recognized in terms of faith, hope, and charity.)

Fourth Rule: Spiritual desolation. I call desolation the contrary of what I have just described. It is darkness of the soul, interior turmoil, an inclination to what is base and material, a restlessness caused by different anxieties and temptations out of which comes a loss of all confidence in God, and leaves it without hope, without love. In this state the soul is listless, unaffected, sad, and, as it were, separated from its Creator and Lord. Just as consolation is the contrary of desolation, the thoughts that come from consolation are the opposite of the thoughts that owe their origin to desolation.

Fifth Rule. In times of desolation, one should never change anything but should continue on following resolutely and firmly the decisions and choices he made on the preceding day or at the time when, during his last consolation, he supported the choice he already made. The reason for this is that if it is, above all, the good spirit who guides and counsels us in consolation, then it is the evil spirit who guides and counsels us in desolation, and his counsels can lead us only to spiritual dead ends.

Sixth Rule. If in desolation we should not change our former resolutions, then it is best for us to be resolute on changing ourselves so as to face desolation. For example, we will anchor ourselves even deeper in prayer and meditation, and we will examine ourselves seriously, and we will make more room for penance, without going beyond what is prudent and always under the scrutiny of our director.

Seventh Rule. The one who is in desolation ought to think about the fact that to test him the Lord has left him to his own natural resources in order that he might resist the different anxieties and temptations from Satan. For resist he can, with the divine help that is always within his grasp, even if he does not clearly feel it. The fact is that the Lord has taken back from him his enthusiastic fervor, the feeling of his love, the intense realization of his grace; however, he has left him with grace sufficient for his eternal salvation.

Eighth Rule. The person who is in desolation should force himself to continue on in patience and face the problems that assail him. Let him reflect on the fact that he will soon find consolation if he uses the means that were described in the sixth rule against this desolation.

Ninth Rule. There are three principal causes for desolation:

The *first* is that we are halfhearted, listless, or negligent in making our spiritual exercises. As a result consolation is withdrawn from us.

The *second* is that God may want us to see how good we really are and how far we are able to go in his service and praise without being supported by consolations and graces of fervor.

The *third* is that God may wish to have us become aware of ourselves and to prove to ourselves that it is in no way within our power to generate or to foster a true devotion, an intense love, tears, or any other kind of spiritual consolation, but that everything is a gratuitous gift from his hand. Therefore he does not want us "to lay our eggs in some other bird's nest", becoming filled with the spirit of pride or vainglory and attributing to ourselves devotion or spiritual consolation (see Judg 7:2–3).

Tenth rule. The person who is in consolation ought to think of how he will conduct himself later during the time when desolation returns, and from these thoughts he ought to gain new strength that he can use during the time of desolation.

Eleventh rule. The person who is in consolation ought to do his best to live in humility as much as he can. He should think from time to time how helpless he is during the time of desolation when he is deprived of this grace of consolation. The person who is in desolation, on the contrary, ought to tell himself that he can do much with grace, and that what he has is sufficient for him to resist all his enemies, providing he draw his strength from his Creator and Lord.

St. Francis de Sales goes so far as to say that humility (the sense of our spiritual weakness) is morbid and harmful if it is not accompanied by "generosity" (courage that relies on strength from God).

Twelfth rule. Satan behaves like someone with a cowardly personality. He is weak when we resist him and strong when we let him have his way. He gives way, loses his self-assurance, and runs off with his temptations when the person relies on spiritual principles to face Satan's attacks with decision, and acts in the diametrically opposite way that the enemy suggests. But if under the assault of temptations the person begins to show fear and loses his courage, there is no beast on the face of the earth more ferocious than the enemy of our human nature in his relentlessness to pursue with monstrous perversity his evil designs.

Thirteenth rule. Satan also behaves like a frivolous lover who likes to carry on in a secret way so as not to be discovered. A flirtatious man who makes passes at the daughter of an honorable father or the wife of an upright man by his falsehearted talk desires that his words and way of acting be kept secret. He becomes quite upset when the daughter tells her father or the wife tells her husband about his insinuating words and his depraved designs. He will fast come to the conclusion that he will not carry off his intentions without difficulty.

In the same way when the enemy of our human nature succeeds in introducing his ruses and insinuations to an upright soul, he asks nothing more than to have these received in secret and kept in the dark. But when the person tells these to a good confessor or to some other spiritual person, our enemy becomes very annoyed. He clearly realizes that he cannot succeed in his perverted undertaking, seeing that his deceptions are so base that they can only be defeated.

Fourteenth rule. Finally, Satan behaves like a military leader intent on conquering and capturing a fortified city. After he establishes his own camp, he carefully reconnoiters the city's fortifications and the disposition of its troops, and then he makes his attacks at the weakest point.

The enemy of our human nature acts in the same way. He makes his rounds about us, inspecting all our virtues, theological, cardinal, and moral. At that place where he discovers we are weakest and most insecure in what pertains to our eternal salvation, he attacks us, hoping to take us by surprise.

Rules for a Better Discernment
of the Movements of the Soul

First rule.

It is characteristic of God and his angels, when they act upon the soul, to give it true spiritual joy, in banishing all sadness or trouble that Satan prompts within us.[1]

It is characteristic of Satan to fight against this happiness and spiritual consolation by continuously suggesting to the soul false reasons, subtleties, and specious arguments.

Second rule. God our Lord alone is able to give to the soul consolation without any previous cause. In fact, it is proper to the Creator to enter the soul, to leave it, to excite within it movements that draw it totally to the love of his Divine Majesty.

I say without cause—that is, without any preceding feeling or understanding of any subject by which the soul on its own could incite consolation in the understanding or will.

This rule is considered one of the major criteria for an authentic action of the Holy Spirit.

Third rule. Let us suppose that this preceding cause exists. Beginning with this, the good as well as the evil angel is able to console the soul, but for different purposes. The good angel consoles the soul to make it progress that it may grow and rise from the good to the better; the bad angel consoles it for contrary purposes and also that he might draw it in the end to his own perverse designs.

Fourth rule. It is the tactics of the bad angel, as he disguises himself as the angel of light, to begin by going along with the just

[1] These rules are more properly designed for the retreatant during the Second Week, but they can be helpful for anyone committed to living a more Christian life.

soul and then at last to have him travel along his own path. In the beginning, he proposes holy and wholesome thoughts that are in harmony with the just soul's way of thinking, and then, bit by bit, he tries to bring him around to his purposes by enticing the soul to fall into uncharted snares and lead him along perverse ways.

Fifth rule. We must pay special attention to our thoughts. If the beginning, middle, and end are all good and are directed to what is wholly good, it is a sign of the good angel. But if during the course of our thoughts the soul hits up against something that is evil or sensuous, or less good than what had been suggested to it in the beginning, or if these thoughts weaken the soul, disturb it, trouble it, and strip it of peace, tranquility, and quiet that it had before, it is a clear sign that these thoughts come from the evil spirit, that enemy of our progress and of our eternal salvation.

Sixth rule. When the enemy of human nature has been unmasked and recognized by "his serpent's tail" (this bad end to which he is leading us), it will be profitable for the person whom he has seduced to go back over and think about the sequence of good thoughts that Satan had suggested to him, how they began, and then how, bit by bit, he used them to make him lose the spiritual joy that he had found, until at last he brought him around to his perverse plan. This way, thanks to this experience duly analyzed and well stored in his memory, the person will know how to guard himself in the future against the demon's customary traps.

Seventh rule. The good angel touches souls who are going from good to better sweetly, lightly, gently, just as when a drop of water penetrates into a sponge. The bad angel touches them in a stinging way, that is to say, with noise and agitation: just as when a drop of water splashes on a stone. It is the opposite with souls who go from bad to worse. The reason is obvious: Are not the dispositions of the soul like or unlike the personality characteristics of the angel? When there is a clash of interests, the angel enters the soul with commotion, and the soul easily perceives the angel's presence; when there is an agreement of interests, the angel enters without a fracas as if he is coming into his own home with the doors wide open.

Eighth rule.   As we have already stated, when the consolation is without any preceding cause, there can be no risk of a trap because it can come only from God our Lord. However, a spiritual person to whom God has given this consolation ought to consider it observantly and distinguish attentively between the time of the consolation and the time following, that is, while the soul is still inflamed by the lingering grace from the consolation. The fact is that during this second period (when the soul is yet enjoying the aftereffects of the consolation) it often forms different projects or resolutions that are not inspired immediately by God our Lord. These notions may come either as a consequence of the soul's own reasoning and judgments or from the influence of the good or bad spirit. At any rate, they should be carefully scrutinized before they are fully credited and put into execution.

Some Helpful Guidelines on How
to Recognize and Deal with Scruples

Preliminary note.   Scruples can be simply a psychological disability, but this does not make them any less painful. Clearly their cure is within the purview of a medical doctor or a psychologist. But, in addition to therapy, it is a good practice to have regular, first-rate spiritual direction, which in general should be based on absolute obedience on the part of the scrupulous person to his spiritual director. We do not want to say anything here about scruples that are pathological in nature. However, in cases of purely religious scruples, we should not forget that a person's temperament and his fatigue factor almost inevitably play important roles.

First note.   Sometimes we name something a scruple that in fact has its origin in our judgment or in our ignorance. On my own authority, I decide something is a sin that is not a sin. For example, by chance I walk over two pieces of straw in the form of a cross, and I judge that that is a sin. This is a case of faulty judgment, not a scruple.

Second note.   After walking on this cross, or after I think, say, or do anything else, the idea may come to me, from without, as it were, that I am guilty of sin. Then it may seem to me that I have not sinned. But I do feel troubled. I both doubt and do not doubt at the same time, and I do not come to a decision. That is a real scruple. The scruple can come from a weakness or even a disease in the personality; it can also be the action of the devil. In either case, it is a difficult trial for the soul.

Third note.   The pseudoscruple described in the first note should be abhorred. Everything about it is false. For a time, it is possible the scruple described in the second note could be helpful to the soul that has given up its spiritual exercises. It may greatly purify such a soul by freeing it from even the appearance of sin. According to St. Gregory's dictum: "It is the achievement of delicate souls *in a certain sense* to see a fault where there is none."

Fourth note.   Satan keeps a watchful eye on the soul, determining if it is blunted or sensitive. If sensitive, he works to the point of making it excessively refined so that he can more easily trouble it and upset it. For example, if he sees that the soul does not consent to committing either a mortal or a venial sin, nor does it entertain anything that even appears to be deliberately sinful, he tries to make it imagine sins where there are none present—for example, in some word or thought that has absolutely no importance whatsoever.

Does Satan busy himself in the opposite way with a blunted mind? Here he attempts to make the soul even more blunted. For example, if the soul pays no attention to venial sins, he will encourage it to pay little heed to mortal sins. If before it had some fear of a mortal sin, he will try to minimize or even do away altogether with such fears.

Fifth note.   The soul that desires to make progress in the spiritual life ought always to take the opposite course to that proposed by Satan. If he seeks to make the soul more blunted, it should apply itself to making itself more sensitive. If he tries to supersensitize the soul, it must force itself to become tougher so as to establish itself between these extremes, where it can enjoy perfect peace.

Sixth note.   It can happen that a soul might earnestly want to do something in accord with the Church or the desires of superiors, something that would be for the glory of God our Lord. But then, under the pretext of avoiding vainglory or for some other religious reason, it would hesitate to speak up or to do what it had thought of doing. Under these circumstances the soul ought to lift up its spirit toward its Creator and Lord, and if it sees that what it is about to say or do is indeed for his service, or at least not contrary to his service, it ought to act in the exact opposite way from the temptation, saying to the Tempter with St. Bernard: "I did not begin this undertaking for you, and it is not for you that I will put it aside."

Suggested Schedule for an Eight-Day Retreat

It could happen that a person would want to make the Spiritual Exercises but could only devote eight days to following the prescribed meditations and contemplations. He should be assured that even in eight days he can profit greatly from these Spiritual Exercises.[1]

Such a person should follow this eight-day schedule of meditations or contemplations:

1st day: the Foundation (and chapter 1 of the Letter to the Ephesians) (pp. 59–65)

2nd day: my personal sins and the Colloquy of Mercy (pp. 71–77)

3rd day: the contemplation of the Kingdom (pp. 87–97)

4th day: the Incarnation (pp. 98–102)

5th day: the Meditation on Two Standards (and the three degrees of humility) (pp. 115–25)

6th day: the Last Supper and the institution of the Holy Eucharist (pp. 164–68)

7th day: the Passion of our Lord (pp. 169–86)

8th day: the Resurrection of our Lord (pp. 188–192)

This eight-day retreat will be more successful if the retreatant does spend some time making the Contemplation to Attain the Love of God (pp. 204–8). St. Ignatius suggested that this contemplation could be made at any time during the course of the thirty-day retreat.

---

[1] The advice and recommendations given to the retreatant making the thirty-day retreat remain the same for those making this eight-day retreat.